Data Science & Gene

Interview Questions

A comprehensive collection of interview questions and

answers covering data science, machine learning,

and generative AI concepts.

Generated on: March 30, 2025

Table of Contents

Data Science Fundamentals

Q: Python program to show how to add elements to an array

A: **Adding Elements to an Array in Python**

==

Python provides several ways to add elements to an array. Here, we'll explore the most common methods using the `list` data structure, which is the equivalent of an array in Python.

Method 1: Using the `append()` Method

The `append()` method adds a single element to the end of the array.

```python
# Initialize an empty array
array = []

# Add elements to the array using
append() array.append(1)
array.append(2) array.append(3)

print(array)  # Output: [1, 2,
3] ```
```

Method 2: Using the `extend()` Method

The `extend()` method adds multiple elements to the end of the array.

```python
# Initialize an empty array
array = []
```

```
# Add multiple elements to the array using extend()
array.extend([1, 2, 3])

print(array)  # Output: [1, 2, 3]
```

Method 3: Using the `insert()` Method

The `insert()` method adds a single element at a specified position in

the array.

```python
# Initialize an array array
= [1, 3]

# Add an element at a specified position using insert() array. Insert

(1, 2)

print(array)  # Output: [1, 2, 3]
```

Method 4: Using the `+` Operator

The `+` operator can be used to concatenate two arrays.

```python
# Initialize two arrays
array1 = [1, 2] array2
= [3, 4]

# Concatenate the arrays using the + operator array =
array1 + array2

print(array)  # Output: [1, 2, 3, 4]
```

Example Use Case

Here's an example use case that demonstrates how to add

elements to an array in a real-world scenario:

```python
def add_student(students, name, grade):
    """
    Add a student to the list of students.

    Args:
        students (list): The list of students.
        name (str): The name of the student.
        grade (int): The grade of the student.
    """
    student = {"name": name, "grade": grade}
    students.append(student)

# Initialize an empty list of students
students = []

# Add students to the list
add_student(students, "John Doe", 90)
add_student(students, "Jane Doe", 85)

# Print the list of students
print(students)
# Output: [{'name': 'John Doe', 'grade': 90}, {'name': 'Jane Doe', 'grade': 85}]
```

In this example, we define a function `add_student()` that adds a

student to the list of students using the `append()` method.

We then initialize an empty list of students and add two students

to the list using the `add_student()` function. Finally,

we print the list of students to verify that the students were

added correctly.

Q: Python program to show how to remove elements from a Python array

A: **Removing Elements from a Python Array**

==

Python provides several ways to remove elements from an array.

Here are a few methods:

Method 1: Using the `remove()` method

The `remove()` method removes the first occurrence of the specified element.

```python
# Define an array
array = [1, 2, 3, 4, 5]

# Remove the element 3
array.remove(3) print(array) #
Output: [1, 2, 4, 5]
```

Method 2: Using the `pop()` method

The `pop()` method removes the element at the specified position.

```python
# Define an array
array = [1, 2, 3, 4, 5]

# Remove the element at index 2 array.pop(2)

print(array) # Output: [1, 2, 4, 5]
```

Method 3: Using list comprehension

List comprehension provides a concise way to create a new list without certain elements.

```python
# Define an array
array = [1, 2, 3, 4, 5]

# Remove the element 3
array = [x for x in array if x != 3]

print(array)  # Output: [1, 2, 4, 5]
```

Method 4: Using the `del` statement

The `del` statement can be used to remove an element at a

specific index.

```python
# Define an array array
= [1, 2, 3, 4, 5]

# Remove the element at index 2
del array[2] print(array)  #

Output: [1, 2, 4, 5]
```

Method 5: Using the `numpy` library

If you're working with large arrays, you may want to consider

using the `numpy` library, which provides an efficient way

to remove elements.

```python    import
numpy as np

# Define an array
array = np.array([1, 2, 3, 4, 5])

# Remove the element 3
array = np.delete(array, np.where(array == 3))
```

print(array) # Output: [1 2 4 5] ```

Example Use Case

Suppose you have a list of exam scores and you want to remove any

scores that are below a certain threshold.

```python
# Define a list of exam scores scores
= [90, 80, 70, 60, 50]

# Remove any scores below 70
scores = [x for x in scores if x >= 70]

print(scores)  # Output: [90, 80, 70]
```

Q: Python program to check if a number is prime

or not

A: **Prime Number Checker in Python**

=======================================

Overview

This program checks if a given number is prime or not. A prime

number is a natural number greater than 1 that has no positive

divisors other than 1 and itself.

Code
```python def
is_prime(n):
    """
    Checks if a number is prime.

    Args:       n (int): The number
to check.
```

Returns:
    bool: True if the number is prime, False otherwise.
    """ if
n <= 1:
    return False   for i in range(2,
int(n ** 0.5) + 1):   if n % i == 0:
return False   return True

```
def main():
    num = int(input("Enter a number: "))    if is_prime(num):
        print(f"{num} is a prime number.")
    else:    print(f"{num} is not a prime number.")


if __name__ == "__main__":
    main() ```
```

Explanation

1. The `is_prime` function takes an integer `n` as input and checks if it'sprime.
2. If `n` is less than or equal to 1, it's not prime, so we return False.
3. We only need to check divisors up to the square root of `n`, as any factorlarger than that would have a corresponding factor smaller than the square root.
4. We use a for loop to iterate from 2 to the square root of `n` (inclusive) and check if `n` is divisible by any of these numbers. If it is, we return False.
5. If `n` is not divisible by any of these numbers, we return True, Indicating that it's prime.
6. In the `main` function, we take user input, check if the

   number is primeusing the `is_prime` function, and print the result.

Example Use Cases

* Enter a prime number: 23Output: 23 is a prime number.
* Enter a non-prime number: 30Output: 30 is not a prime number.

 * Enter a special case: 1
Output: 1 is not a prime number.

Q: Python program to check if the given string is a palindrome

A: **Palindrome Checker in Python**
=====================================

A palindrome is a string that reads the same backwards as

forwards. Here's a simple Python program that checks if a

given string is a palindrome:

```python
```python def is_palindrome(s:
str) -> bool:
    """
    Checks if the given string is a palindrome.

    Args:        s (str): The
input string.

    Returns:
    bool: True if the string is a palindrome, False otherwise.
    """
    s = ''.join(c for c in s if c.isalnum()).lower()  # Remove
non-alphanumeric characters and convert to lowercase
    return s == s[::-1]  # Compare the string with its reverse

# Example usage:
def main():
    strings = ["radar", "hello", "A man, a plan, a canal: Panama"]    for
s in strings:
        print(f"'{s}' is a palindrome: {is_palindrome(s)}")
if __name__ ==
"__main__":    main() ```
```

How it works:

1. The `is_palindrome` function takes a string `s` as input.
```

2. It removes non-alphanumeric characters from the string using agenerator expression and converts the string to lowercase using the `lower()` method.
3. It then compares the resulting string with its reverse using slicing

(`s[::-1]`).

4. If the string is equal to its reverse, the function returns

   `True`, indicatingthat the string is a palindrome. Otherwise,

   it returns `False`.

Example output:

```
'radar' is a palindrome: True
'hello' is a palindrome: False
'A man, a plan, a canal: Panama' is a palindrome: True
```

Q: Python program to get the factorial of a number

A: **Factorial Program in Python**

=================================

Description

This program calculates the factorial of a given integer using

a recursive function and an iterative method.

Code

```python              def
factorial_recursive(n):
    """
    Calculate the factorial of a number using recursion.

    Args:
        n (int): The input number.
    Returns:
        int: The factorial of the input number.
```

```
    """    if n == 0:       return 1    else:
    return n * factorial_recursive(n-1)


def factorial_iterative(n):
    """
    Calculate the factorial of a number using iteration.

    Args:       n (int): The input
number.

    Returns:
        int: The factorial of the input number.
    """    result = 1    for i
in range(1, n + 1):
        result    *=    i
    return result


def main():
    num = int(input("Enter a  number: "))
    if num < 0:
        print("Factorial is not defined for negative numbers.")    else:
        print(f"Factorial (recursive) of {num}:


{factorial_recursive(num)}")


        print(f"Factorial (iterative) of {num}: {factorial_iterative(num)}")


    if __name__ == "__main__":
    main() ```
```

Explanation

* The `factorial_recursive` function uses recursion to calculate the factorial of a number. It checks if the input number is 0 (the base case) and returns

1. Otherwise, it calls itself with the input number decremented by 1 and multiplies the result by the current number.

* The `factorial_iterative` function uses a loop to calculate the
* factorial of anumber. It initializes a variable `result` to 1 and then
* iterates from 1 to the input number, multiplying `result` by each
* number in the range.
* The `main` function takes user input, checks if the

* number is negative,and then calls both the recursive

  and iterative functions to calculate the factorial.

  ### Example Use Case

* Run the program and enter a positive integer (e.g., 5).
* The program will output the factorial of the input number using

  bothrecursive and iterative methods.

Example output:
```

Enter a number: 5
Factorial (recursive) of 5: 120
Factorial (iterative) of 5: 120
```

Q: [4,5,6,7,2,3,11,13] Sort the element in a such a way
that have even should come first and odd numbers at last

A: To sort the elements in such a way that even numbers come first

and odd numbers come last, we can use a custom sorting approach.

Here's the step-by-step process:

1. Separate the even and odd numbers:
   Even numbers: [4, 6, 2]
   Odd numbers: [5, 7, 3, 11, 13]

2. Sort the even numbers in ascending order: [2, 4, 6]
3. Sort the odd numbers in ascending order: [3, 5, 7, 11, 13]

4. Combine the sorted even and odd numbers: [2, 4, 6, 3, 5, 7, 11, 13]

So, the final sorted array is: [2, 4, 6, 3, 5, 7, 11, 13]

Q: python Program to reverse a string

A: **Reversing a String in Python**
==================================

Here's a simple Python program that takes a string as input

and returns the reversed string.

Method 1: Using Slicing

```python
def
reverse_st
ring(s):
    """Return    the    reversed
string."""    return s[::-1]

# Example usage
input_str  =  "Hello,  World!"
print("Original        string:",
input_str)
print("Reversed string:", reverse_string(input_str))
```

Method 2: Using the `reversed` Function

```python
def
reverse_st
ring(s):
    """Return    the    reversed
string."""                return
"".join(reversed(s))

# Example usage
input_str  =  "Hello,  World!"
print("Original        string:",
input_str)
print("Reversed string:", reverse_string(input_str))
```

Method 3: Using a Loop

```python
def
reverse_st
ring(s):
    """Return the
reversed string."""
reversed_str = ""    for
char in s:
        reversed_str    =    char    +
reversed_str    return reversed_str

# Example usage
input_str = "Hello, World!" print("Original
string:", input_str) print("Reversed
string:", reverse_string(input_str))
```

Method 4: Using the `reduce` Function

```python
from functools import reduce

def reverse_string(s):
    """Return the reversed string."""    return
reduce(lambda x, y: y + x, s)

# Example usage
input_str = "Hello, World!" print("Original
string:", input_str)
print("Reversed string:", reverse_string(input_str))
```

All of these methods will output:
```

Original string: Hello, World!
Reversed string: !dlroW ,olleH
```

Note: The slicing method (`s[::-1]`) is generally

the most efficient and Pythonic way to reverse a string.

Q: Write a Python program to find the sum of the first n natural numbers

A: **Natural Number Sum Calculator**

==

This Python program calculates the sum of the first n

natural numbers using a simple formula.

Code

```python
                          def
sum_of_natural_numbers(n):
    """
    Calculate the sum of the first n natural numbers.
    Args:
        n (int): The number of natural numbers to sum.

    Returns:
        int: The sum of the first n natural numbers.
    """
if  n <=
0:
        raise ValueError("n must be a positive integer")
    return n * (n + 1) // 2

def main():
    # Example usage:
    n = int(input("Enter a positive integer: "))
    try:
        result = sum_of_natural_numbers(n)
        print(f"The sum of the first {n} natural numbers is:
{result}")    except ValueError as e:
        print(e)

if __name__ ==
"__main__":    main() ```
```

Explanation

The `sum_of_natural_numbers` function takes an integer `n` as

input and returns the sum of the first `n` natural numbers.

The formula used is `n * (n + 1) / 2`, which is a well-known

mathematical formula for calculating the sum of an arithmetic

series.

The `main` function demonstrates how to use
the `sum_of_natural_numbers` function. It prompts the user to
enter a positive integer, calculates the sum, and prints the result.
If the user enters a non-positive integer, it catches the `ValueError` exception
and prints an error message.
Example Use Cases

----

*   Enter `5` to calculate the sum of the first 5 natural numbers:
`1 + 2 + 3 + 4+ 5 = 15`
*   Enter `10` to calculate the sum of the first 10 natural numbers:

`1 + 2 + 3 +4 + 5 + 6 + 7 + 8 + 9 + 10 = 55`

Note: This program uses integer division (`//`) to ensure that the

result is an integer.

Q: Write a Python program to check if a year is a leap year

A: **Leap Year Checker in Python**
=================================

Description

This program checks if a given year is a leap year or not.

Code

```python
```python def is_leap_year(year: int)
-> bool:
    """

    Checks if a year is a leap year.

    Args:    year (int): The year to
check.

    Returns:
    bool: True if the year is a leap year, False otherwise.
    """

    return year % 4 == 0 and (year % 100 != 0 or year % 400 == 0)


def main():
    # Example usage
    year = int(input("Enter a year: "))    if
is_leap_year(year):
        print(f"{year} is a leap year.")
    else:        print(f"{year} is not a leap
year.")


if    __name__    ==    "__main__":
main()
```

Explanation

*   The `is_leap_year` function takes an integer `year` as input and returns
aboolean indicating whether the year is a leap year or not.
*   A year is a leap year if it is divisible by 4, except for years that are divisibleby
100 but not by 400.
*   The `main` function demonstrates how to use the `is_leap_year` functionby
prompting the user to enter a year and then printing whether the year is a leap
year or not.

Example Use Cases

*   Enter a year that is a leap year (e.g., 2020): The program will print "2020is a
leap year."
```

*   Enter a year that is not a leap year (e.g., 2021): The program will print"2021 is not a leap year."

*   Enter a year that is a century year but not a leap year (e.g., 2100): Theprogram will print "2100 is not a leap year."

*   Enter a year that is a century year and a leap year (e.g., 2000): Theprogram will print "2000 is a leap year."

Q: Write a Python program to sort a list of numbers in ascending order.

A: **Sorting a List of Numbers in Ascending Order**
===

Here's a simple Python program that uses the built-in `sorted()` function to

sort a list of numbers in ascending order.

```python
def sort_numbers(num_list):
    """
    Sorts a list of numbers in ascending order.

    Args:       num_list (list): A list of numbers.

    Returns:
        list: The sorted list of numbers.
    """
    return sorted(num_list)
# Example usage:
numbers = [64, 34, 25, 12, 22, 11, 90]
print("Original list:", numbers)
print("Sorted list:", sort_numbers(numbers))
```

Output:

```
Original list: [64, 34, 25, 12, 22, 11, 90]
Sorted list: [11, 12, 22, 25, 34, 64, 90]
```

Explanation:

1. The `sorted()` function takes a list as input and returns a new sorted list.
2. The `sort_numbers()` function takes a list of numbers as input and returns the sorted list.
In the example usage, we create a list of numbers and print the originallist.
3.   We then call the `sort_numbers()` function with the list of

numbers andprint the sorted list.

Alternative Implementation:
If you want to implement the sorting algorithm manually, you can use a simple sorting algorithm like Bubble Sort or Quick Sort. Here's an example using Bubble Sort:

```python
def bubble_sort(num_list):
    """
    Sorts a list of numbers in ascending order using Bubble Sort.

    Args:        num_list (list): A list of numbers.

    Returns:
        list: The sorted list of numbers.
    """
    n = len(num_list)    for i in range(n):
for j in range(0, n - i - 1):        if num_list[j] > num_list[j + 1]:
            num_list[j], num_list[j + 1] = num_list[j + 1], num_list[j]
    return num_list

# Example usage:
numbers = [64, 34, 25, 12, 22, 11, 90] print("Original list:", numbers)
print("Sorted list:", bubble_sort(numbers))
```

Note: The built-in `sorted()` function is generally faster and more efficient than manual sorting algorithms. However, implementing sorting algorithms manually can be useful for learning and educational purposes.

Q: Write a program that asks the user to input a number and prints whether the number is positive and even, positive and odd, or negative.

A: **Number Classification Program**

======================================

Description

This program asks the user to input a number and prints whether the number is positive and even, positive and odd, or negative.

Code

```python
def classify_number():
    """
    Asks the user to input a number and prints whether the number is positive and even, positive and odd, or negative.
    """
    # Ask the user to input a number
    while True:
        try:
            num = int(input("Please enter a number: "))
            break
        except ValueError:
            print("Invalid input. Please enter a valid integer.")

    # Classify the number
    if num > 0:
        if num % 2 == 0:
            print(f"The number {num} is positive and even.")
        else:
            print(f"The number {num} is positive and odd.")
    elif num < 0:
        print(f"The number {num} is negative.")
    else:
        print(f"The number {num} is zero.")

if __name__ == "__main__":
    classify_number()
```

Example Use Cases

* Input: `10`

Output: `The number 10 is positive and even.`
* Input: `7`
Output: `The number 7 is positive and odd.`
* Input: `-5`
Output: `The number -5 is negative.`
* Input: `0`
Output: `The number 0 is zero.`

How to Run

1. Save   the   code   in   a   file   with   a   `.py`
        extension   (e.g.,
`number_classifier.py`).
2. Open a terminal or command prompt and navigate to the directory whereyou
        saved the file.
3. Run the program by typing `python number_classifier.py`.
4. Follow the prompt to input a number.

Q: Write a program that prints all the numbers from 1 to 10 using a while loop.

A: **While Loop Program in Python**
```python                def
print_numbers():
    # Initialize the counter variable    i =
1

    # Use a while loop to print numbers from 1 to 10    while i <=
10:
        print(i)
        # Increment the counter variable    i
+= 1

# Call the function to print numbers
print_numbers()
```

How the Program Works:

1. The `print_numbers` function initializes a counter variable `i` to 1.
2. The while loop checks if `i` is less than or equal to 10.
3. If the condition is true, the program prints the current value of `i`.
4. The counter variable `i` is incremented by 1 using `i += 1`.

5. Steps 2-4 repeat until `i` exceeds 10.

Example Output:
```
1
2
3
4
5
6
7
8
9
10
```

Q: Write a program that prints a 5x5 grid of asterisks (*) using nested loops.

A: **Printing a 5x5 Grid of Asterisks**
=====================================

Below is a Python program that uses nested loops to print a 5x5 grid of asterisks.

```python
def print_grid(size):
    """
    Prints a size x size grid of asterisks.

    Args:    size (int): The size of the grid.
    """
    for i in range(size):
        for j in range(size):
            print("*", end=" ")
        print()

def main():
    # Define the size of the grid    size = 5

    # Print the grid    print_grid(size)
```

```
if __name__ == "__main__":
main() ```
```

Explanation

----

1. The `print_grid` function takes an integer `size` as input, representing thesize of the grid.
2. The outer loop iterates `size` times, representing the rows of the grid.
3. The inner loop also iterates `size` times, representing the columns of thegrid.
4. Inside the inner loop, an asterisk (`*`) is printed followed by a space. The`end=" "` argument to the `print` function prevents a newline from being printed after each asterisk.
5. After each inner loop iteration (i.e., after each row), a newline is printed tomove to the next row.
6. In the `main` function, the size of the grid is set to 5 and the `print_grid`function is called to print the grid.

Example Output

```
* * * * *
* * * * *
* * * * *
* * * * *
* * * * *
```

Q: Write a program that asks the user to input numbers until they input 0. The program should print the sum of all the input numbers.

A: **Sum of Input Numbers Program**
==================================

Description

This program asks the user to input numbers until they input 0. It then prints the sum of all the input numbers.

Code

```python
def get_user_input():
    """Gets user input until 0 is entered"""
    numbers = []
    while True:
        user_input = input("Enter a number (0 to stop): ")
        try:
            num = float(user_input)
            if num == 0:
                break
            numbers.append(num)
        except ValueError:
            print("Invalid input. Please enter a number.")
    return numbers


def calculate_sum(numbers):
    """Calculates the sum of a list of numbers"""
    return sum(numbers)


def main():
    numbers = get_user_input()
    total_sum = calculate_sum(numbers)
    print(f"The sum of the input numbers is: {total_sum}")


if __name__ == "__main__":
    main()
```

Example Usage

1. Run the program.
2. Enter a number when prompted (e.g., `5`).
3. Continue entering numbers until you want to stop (e.g., `3`, `2`, `1`).
4. Enter `0` to stop inputting numbers.
5. The program will print the sum of all the input numbers (e.g., `11`).

Notes

*   The program uses a `while` loop to continuously ask for user input until `0` is entered.
*   The `get_user_input` function handles invalid input (e.g., non-numericcharacters) by catching `ValueError` exceptions.
*   The `calculate_sum` function uses the built-in `sum` function to calculatethe sum of the input numbers.

*   The `main` function orchestrates the program's logic and prints the finalresult.

Q: Write a program that prints all the numbers from 1 to 10 except 5 using a for loop and continue statement.

A: **Printing Numbers from 1 to 10 Except 5**

===

Below is a Python program that uses a for loop and the continue statement to print all numbers from 1 to 10 except 5.

```python
# Define the range of numbers
start = 1 end =
10

# Iterate over the range of numbers for num
in range(start, end + 1):
    # Check if the number is 5, if so, skip it    if
num == 5:     continue    # Print the number
print(num)
```

How it Works:

1. We define the start and end of the range of numbers we want to print.
2. We use a for loop to iterate over the range of numbers.
3. Inside the loop, we check if the current number is 5.
4. If the number is 5, we use the `continue` statement to skip the rest of thecurrent iteration and move on to the next one.
5. If the number is not 5, we print it.

Example Output:

```
1
2
3
4
6
7
```

8
9
10
```

This program demonstrates how to use the `continue` statement to skip certain iterations in a loop, allowing you to print all numbers from 1 to 10 except 5.

**Q: Write a program that asks the user to input a number and prints all the even numbers from 1 to that number using a for loop.**

A: **Even Number Printer Program**
==================================

### Description

This program asks the user to input a number and prints all the even numbers from 1 to that number using a for loop.

### Code

```python
def print_even_numbers(n):    """
    Prints all the even numbers from 1 to n.

    Args:        n (int): The upper
limit.
    """    for i in range(1, n + 1):
        if i % 2 == 0:        print(i)

def main():
    # Ask the user to input a number
    while True:    try:
        num = int(input("Enter a number: "))        if
num <= 0:
            print("Please enter a positive integer.")        else:
            break        except
ValueError:
        print("Invalid input. Please enter a positive integer.")

    # Print the even numbers
    print("Even numbers from 1 to", num, "are:")    print_even_numbers(num)
```
```

```
if __name__ == "__main__":
    main()
```

Example Usage

When you run this program, it will ask you to enter a number. Let's say you enter `10`. The program will then print all the even numbers from 1 to 10:

```
Enter a number: 10
Even numbers from 1 to 10 are:
2
4
6
8
10
```

How it Works

1. The `print_even_numbers` function takes an integer `n` as input and uses a for loop to iterate from 1 to `n` (inclusive).
2. Inside the loop, it checks if the current number `i` is even by using the modulo operator (`i % 2 == 0`).
3. If `i` is even, it prints the number.
4. The `main` function asks the user to input a number and calls the `print_even_numbers` function with the user's input.
5. The program uses a try-except block to handle invalid inputs and ensures that the user enters a positive integer.

Q: Write a program that calculates the sum of the digits of a number input by the user using a while loop.

A: **Digit Sum Calculator**
==========================

Description

This program calculates the sum of the digits of a number input by the user using a while loop.

Code

```python
def calculate_digit_sum():    #
Get user input
    num = int(input("Enter a number: "))

    # Initialize sum variable    digit_sum =
0

    # Loop through each digit in the number    while
num != 0:
        # Add the last digit to the sum        digit_sum
+= num % 10
        # Remove the last digit from the number        num
//= 10

    # Print the result
    print("The sum of the digits is:", digit_sum)

# Example usage if __name__ ==
"__main__":
    calculate_digit_sum()
```

Explanation

1. The program starts by getting a number input from the user using the `input` function.
2. It initializes a variable `digit_sum` to store the sum of the digits.
3. The program then enters a while loop that continues until all digits havebeen processed (i.e., `num` becomes 0).
4. Inside the loop, the program adds the last digit of the number to the `digit_sum` using the modulo operator (`num % 10`).
5. It then removes the last digit from the number using integer division(`num //= 10`).
6. Once all digits have been processed, the program prints the final sum ofthe digits.

Example Use Cases

* Input: `1234`
Output: `The sum of the digits is: 10`
* Input: `56789`
Output: `The sum of the digits is: 35`

Q: Write a function to reverse a linked list.

A: ### Reversing a Linked List ####
Function Description

The following function, `reverse_linked_list`, takes the head of a linked list as input and returns the head of the reversed linked list.

Code

```python
class Node:
    """Node class representing a node in the linked list."""
    def __init__(self, data):
        self.data = data
        self.next = None


class LinkedList:
    """Linked list class with a method to reverse the list."""
    def __init__(self):
        self.head = None

    def append(self, data):
        """Append a node to the end of the linked list."""
        new_node = Node(data)
        if not self.head:
            self.head = new_node
            return
        current = self.head
        while current.next:
            current = current.next
        current.next = new_node

    def reverse(self):
        """Reverse the linked list."""
        prev_node = None
        current_node = self.head
        while current_node:
            next_node = current_node.next
            current_node.next = prev_node
            prev_node = current_node
            current_node = next_node
        self.head = prev_node

    def print_list(self):
        """Print the linked list."""
```

```
current = self.head      while
current:
        print(current.data, end=" ")
current = current.next      print()
```

```
# Example usage:
linked_list = LinkedList() linked_list.append(1)
linked_list.append(2) linked_list.append(3)
linked_list.append(4) linked_list.append(5)

print("Original Linked List:")

linked_list.print_list() linked_list.reverse()

print("Reversed Linked List:")
linked_list.print_list() ```
```

Explanation

1.   We start by defining a `Node` class to represent each node in the linkedlist, containing `data` and a reference to the `next` node.
2.   The `LinkedList` class has methods to `append` nodes, `reverse` the list,and `print_list` to display the linked list.
3.   In   the   `reverse`   method,   we   initialize   three   pointers: `prev_node`,`current_node`, and `next_node`. We traverse the linked list, reversing the `next` pointer of each node.
4.   Finally, we update the `head` of the linked list to point to the new firstnode, which is the last node in the original list.

Time Complexity

*   The time complexity of the `reverse` function is O(n), where n is thenumber of nodes in the linked list, since we traverse the list once.
*   The space complexity is O(1), as we only use a constant amount ofspace to store the pointers.

Q: Given a string, find the first non-repeating character

A: **Solution: Finding the First Non-Repeating Character in a String**

Problem Statement

Given a string, find the first non-repeating character.

Approach

To solve this problem, we can use a dictionary to store the frequency of each character in the string. Then, we can iterate through the string again to find the first character with a frequency of 1.

Code

```python
def find_first_non_repeating_char(s):
    """
    Finds the first non-repeating character in a string.

    Args:        s (str): The input string.

    Returns:
        str: The first non-repeating character, or None if no such character exists.
    """
    # Create a dictionary to store the frequency of each character
    char_freq = {}    for char in s:        if char in char_freq:
            char_freq[char] += 1
    else:        char_freq[char] = 1

    # Find the first non-repeating character
    for char in s:        if char_freq[char] == 1:
    return char

    # If no non-repeating character is found, return None        return None

# Example usage s =
"aabbc"
result = find_first_non_repeating_char(s)
print(result) # Output: c
```

Explanation

1. Create a dictionary `char_freq` to store the frequency of each characterin the string.

2. Iterate through the string to populate the `char_freq` dictionary.
3. Iterate through the string again to find the first character with a frequency of 1.
4. If a non-repeating character is found, return it. Otherwise, return None.

Time Complexity

The time complexity of this solution is O(n), where n is the length of the input string. This is because we need to iterate through the string twice: once to populate the `char_freq` dictionary and once to find the first non-repeating character.

Space Complexity

The space complexity of this solution is O(n), where n is the length of the input string. This is because we need to store the frequency of each character in the `char_freq` dictionary. In the worst case, all characters in the string are unique, so the size of the dictionary will be equal to the length of the string.

Q: Implement a stack using a list in Python.

A: ### Implementing a Stack using a List in Python ####
Overview

A stack is a linear data structure that follows the LIFO (Last In, First Out) principle. This means that the last item added to the stack will be the first one to be removed.

Code Implementation

```python
class Stack:
    def __init__(self):
        """
        Initializes an empty stack.
        """
        self.stack = []

    def push(self, item):
        """
        Adds an item to the top of the stack.

        Args:
            item (any): The item to be added to the stack.
        """
        self.stack.append(item)
```

```python
def pop(self):
    """

    Removes and returns the item from the top of the stack.

    Returns:
        any: The item removed from the stack.

    Raises:
        IndexError: If the stack is empty.
    """
    if not self.is_empty():
        return self.stack.pop()
    else:
        raise IndexError("Stack is empty")

def peek(self):
    """

    Returns the item from the top of the stack without removing it.

    Returns:
        any: The item at the top of the stack.

    Raises:
        IndexError: If the stack is empty.
    """
    if not self.is_empty():
        return self.stack[-1]
    else:
        raise IndexError("Stack is empty")

def is_empty(self):
    """

    Checks if the stack is empty.

    Returns:
        bool: True if the stack is empty, False otherwise.
    """
    return len(self.stack) == 0

def size(self):
    """

    Returns the number of items in the stack.
```

Returns:

int: The number of items in the stack.

"""

return len(self.stack)

```
# Example usage: if __name__ ==
"__main__":
    stack = Stack()
    print(stack.is_empty()) # Output: True
stack.push(1)    stack.push(2)    stack.push(3)
    print(stack.size()) # Output: 3    print(stack.peek()) #
Output: 3    print(stack.pop()) # Output: 3
print(stack.size()) # Output: 2
    print(stack.is_empty()) # Output: False
```

Explanation

*   The `Stack` class is initialized with an empty list `stack`.
*   The `push` method adds an item to the top of the stack using the`append` method
    of the list.
*   The `pop` method removes and returns the item from the top of the stackusing
    the `pop` method of the list. It raises an `IndexError` if the stack is empty.
*   The `peek` method returns the item from the top of the stack withoutremoving it.
    It raises an `IndexError` if the stack is empty.
*   The `is_empty` method checks if the stack is empty by checking thelength of the
    list.
*   The `size` method returns the number of items in the stack by returningthe length
    of the list.

Time Complexity

*   `push`: O(1)
*   `pop`: O(1)
*   `peek`: O(1)
*   `is_empty`: O(1)*   `size`: O(1)

Space Complexity

*   O(n), where n is the number of items in the stack.

Q: square the list of numbers

A: You didn't provide a list of numbers. Please provide the list, and I'll be happy to square each number for you.

Once you provide the list, I'll get started.

Q: list comprensation operation with iteration expression for item in iteration

A: **List Comprehension with Iteration Expression**

A list comprehension in Python is a concise way to create a new list by performing an operation on each item in an existing list or other iterable. The general syntax is:

```python
new_list = [expression for item in iterable]
```

Here, `expression` is the operation you want to perform on each item, and `item` is the variable that takes the value of each item in the `iterable` on each iteration.

Example: Squaring Numbers

Suppose you have a list of numbers and you want to create a new list with their squares:

```python
numbers = [1, 2, 3, 4, 5] squares = [x**2 for x
in numbers] print(squares)  # Output: [1, 4, 9,
16, 25]
```

In this example, `x**2` is the expression, and `x` is the variable that takes the value of each item in `numbers` on each iteration.

Example: Filtering Items

You can also add a condition to filter items:

```python
numbers = [1, 2, 3, 4, 5]
even_numbers = [x for x in numbers if x % 2 == 0] print(even_numbers)  #
Output: [2, 4]
```

```
```

Here, `x % 2 == 0` is the condition that filters out odd numbers.

Example: Nested Loops

You can also use nested loops to iterate over multiple iterables:

```python
numbers = [1, 2, 3]
letters = ['a', 'b', 'c']
pairs = [(x, y) for x in numbers for y in letters] print(pairs)
# Output: [(1, 'a'), (1, 'b'), (1, 'c'), (2, 'a'), (2, 'b'), (2, 'c'), (3, 'a'), (3, 'b'), (3, 'c')]
```

In this example, the outer loop iterates over `numbers`, and the inner loop iterates over `letters`. The expression `(x, y)` creates a tuple with the current values of `x` and `y`.

Best Practices

* Use meaningful variable names to make your code readable.
* Keep your list comprehensions concise and focused on a single operation.* Avoid complex conditions or nested loops that can make your code hard to understand.

By following these guidelines, you can write efficient and readable list comprehensions that simplify your code and improve your productivity.

Q: getting unique column using pandas

A: To get unique columns using pandas, you can use the `nunique()` function, which returns the number of unique elements in each column. Here's an example:

```python
import pandas as pd

# Create a sample DataFrame
data = {
    'A': [1, 2, 2, 3, 4, 4, 4],
    'B': [5, 6, 6, 7, 8, 8, 8],
    'C': [9, 10, 10, 11, 12, 12, 12]
}
```

```
df = pd.DataFrame(data)

# Get unique columns unique_columns =
df.nunique()

print(unique_columns)
```

In this example, `unique_columns` will be a pandas Series where the index is the column name and the value is the number of unique elements in that column.

If you want to get the columns with only unique values (i.e., no duplicates), you can use the following code:

```python
unique_columns = df.loc[:, df.nunique() == df.shape[0]]
```

This will return a new DataFrame with only the columns that have unique values.

Alternatively, if you want to get the columns with at least one duplicate value, you can use the following code:

```python
duplicate_columns = df.loc[:, df.nunique() < df.shape[0]]
```

This will return a new DataFrame with only the columns that have at least one duplicate value.

Example Use Cases

*   Data cleaning: You can use `nunique()` to identify columns with duplicatevalues and remove them if necessary.
*   Data exploration: You can use `nunique()` to get an overview of theuniqueness of each column in your dataset.
*   Feature engineering: You can use `nunique()` to identify columns withunique values and use them as features in your machine learning model.

Time Complexity

The time complexity of `nunique()` is O(n), where n is the number of elements in the column. This is because `nunique()` has to iterate over all elements in the column to count the unique values.

Space Complexity

The space complexity of `nunique()` is O(1), because it only returns a single value (the number of unique elements) and does not create any new data structures.

Q: Write a Python program to find the largest number in a list.

A: **Largest Number in a List**
===========================

This Python program finds the largest number in a given list of numbers.

Code
```python
def find_largest_number(num_list):
    """
    Finds the largest number in a list.

    Args:
        num_list (list): A list of numbers.

    Returns:
        int: The largest number in the list.
    """
    return max(num_list)
def main():
    # Example list of numbers
    numbers = [4, 2, 9, 6, 5, 1, 8, 3, 7]

    # Find the largest number
    largest_number = find_largest_number(numbers)

    # Print the result
    print(f"The largest number in the list is: {largest_number}")

if __name__ == "__main__":
    main()
```

Explanation

1. The `find_largest_number` function takes a list of numbers as input andreturns the largest number using the built-in `max` function.
2. In the `main` function, we create a sample list of numbers and call the`find_largest_number` function to find the largest number.
3. The result is then printed to the console.

Example Output
```
The largest number in the list is: 9
```

Running the Code

Save this code to a file (e.g., `largest_number.py`) and run it using Python (e.g., `python largest_number.py`). The program will output the largest number in the example list. You can modify the `numbers` list in the `main` function to test the program with different inputs.

Q: Write a Python program to check if a character is a vowel or consonant.

A: **Vowel or Consonant Checker**
===================================

Description
This Python program checks if a given character is a vowel or consonant.

Code
```python
def
check_vowel_or_consonant(char):
    """
    Checks if a character is a vowel or consonant.

    Args:    char (str): The character to check.

    Returns:    str: "Vowel" if the character is a vowel, "Consonant" if it's a consonant,
    and "Invalid input" if it's neither.
    """

    vowels = 'aeiouAEIOU'
```

```
    if char in vowels:
return "Vowel"    elif
char.isalpha():
    return "Consonant"
else:    return "Invalid
input"

def main():
   char = input("Enter a character: ")    result =
check_vowel_or_consonant(char)    print(f"The
character '{char}' is a {result}.")

if __name__ == "__main__":
main()
```

Example Use Cases

*   Enter a vowel (e.g., 'a', 'A', 'e', etc.): The program will output "Thecharacter 'a' is a Vowel."
*   Enter a consonant (e.g., 'b', 'B', 'c', etc.): The program will output "Thecharacter 'b' is a Consonant."
*   Enter a non-alphabet character (e.g., '1', '@', '#', etc.): The program willoutput "The character '1' is an Invalid input."

How to Run the Program
1.   Save   the   code   in   a   file   with   a   `.py`
          extension   (e.g.,
`vowel_or_consonant.py`).
2.   Open a terminal or command prompt and navigate to the directorywhere you saved the file.
3.   Type `python vowel_or_consonant.py` to run the program.
4.   Enter a character when prompted, and the program will display theresult.

Q: a = ['king', 'Raj', 'vineeth'] reverse the list
A: **Reversing the List**

You can reverse the list `a` using the following methods:

Method 1: Using slicing

```python
```

```
a = ['king', 'Raj', 'vineeth'] a =
a[::-1]
print(a)  # Output: ['vineeth', 'Raj', 'king'] ```
```

Method 2: Using the `reverse()` method

```python
a = ['king', 'Raj', 'vineeth'] a.reverse()
print(a)  # Output: ['vineeth', 'Raj', 'king'] ```
```

Method 3: Using the `reversed()` function

```python
a = ['king', 'Raj', 'vineeth'] a =
list(reversed(a))
print(a)  # Output: ['vineeth', 'Raj', 'king'] ```
```

Q: a = ['king', 'Raj', 'vineeth'] Reverse each string in the list

A: You can reverse each string in the list using a list comprehension in Python. Here is a simple code snippet to achieve this:

```python
a = ['king', 'Raj', 'vineeth']
reversed_list = [word[::-1] for word in a] print(reversed_list)
```

In this code:

- `word[::-1]` is a slice that steps backwards through the entire string,effectively reversing it.
- The list comprehension `[... for word in a]` applies this reversal to eachword in the list `a`.

When you run this code, it will output:

```python
['gnik', 'jaR', 'hteeniv'] ```
```

Q: convert the numbers to letters input_string = 'a6k5d3'

A: To convert the numbers to letters, we can use the standard ordering of the alphabet where 'a' corresponds to 1, 'b' corresponds to 2, and so on.

Given the input string 'a6k5d3', we can replace the numbers with the corresponding letters as follows:

- 6 corresponds to 'f' (since 'a' is 1, 'b' is 2, ..., 'f' is 6)
- 5 corresponds to 'e'- 3 corresponds to 'c'

So, the resulting string with numbers converted to letters would be: 'afkedc'

Q: convert 22031992,23021996 to day-month-year format

A: To convert the given numbers to day-month-year format, I'll separate them and reformat:

1. 22031992 -> 22-03-1992 (22nd March 1992)
2. 23021996 -> 23-02-1996 (23rd February 1996)

Q: Write a Python function to find a continuous subarray in a list that sums to a given target.

A: **Continuous Subarray with Target Sum**
====================================

Here's a Python function that uses a sliding window approach to find a continuous subarray in a list that sums to a given target.

```python
def find_subarray(nums,
target):
    """
    Find a continuous subarray in a list that sums to a given target.

    Args:
-        nums (list): The input list of numbers.    - target (int): The
target sum.

    Returns:
-        list: The continuous subarray that sums to the target, or
None if no suchsubarray exists.
    """
    for i in range(len(nums)):
        current_sum = 0      for j in
range(i, len(nums)):
```

```
current_sum += nums[j]          if
current_sum == target:
        return nums[i:j+1]      return
None
```

```
# Example usage:
nums = [1, 4, 20, 3, 10, 5] target = 33
result = find_subarray(nums, target) if result:    print(f"Continuous
subarray that sums to {target}: {result}") else:    print(f"No
continuous subarray that sums to {target} found.")
```

This function works by iterating over the list and maintaining a running sum of the current subarray. If the running sum equals the target, it returns the current subarray. However, this function has a time complexity of O(n^2) due to the nested loops. For larger lists, a more efficient solution is needed.

Optimized Solution

Here's an optimized solution using a prefix sum array, which reduces the time complexity to O(n).

```python def find_subarray(nums,
target):
    """
    Find a continuous subarray in a list that sums to a given target.

    Args:
    -         nums (list): The input list of numbers.    - target (int): The
    target sum.

    Returns:
    -         list: The continuous subarray that sums to the target, or
    None if no suchsubarray exists.
    """
    prefix_sum = {0: -1}    current_sum
= 0    for i, num in enumerate(nums):
        current_sum += num        if current_sum -
target in prefix_sum:
```

```
    return nums[prefix_sum[current_sum - target] + 1:i+1]
prefix_sum[current_sum] = i    return None

# Example usage:
nums = [1, 4, 20, 3, 10, 5] target = 33
result = find_subarray(nums, target) if result:    print(f"Continuous
subarray that sums to {target}: {result}") else:    print(f"No
continuous subarray that sums to {target} found.")
```

This optimized solution uses a prefix sum array to keep track of the cumulative sum of the list elements. It then checks if the difference between the current sum and the target exists in the prefix sum array. If it does, it returns the corresponding subarray.

Q: how to solve data drift

A: Data drift, also known as concept drift, occurs when the underlying distribution of the data changes over time, causing the performance of a machine learning model to degrade. Solving data drift requires a combination of monitoring, detection, and adaptation strategies. Here are some steps to help you address data drift:

Monitoring

1.   **Track performance metrics**: Regularly monitor the performance ofyour model on a holdout set or a validation set to detect any changes in performance.
2.   **Collect and store data**: Store the data used to train the model, as wellas the data used for prediction, to analyze changes in the data distribution over time.
3.   **Use data quality metrics**: Monitor data quality metrics such as missingvalues, outliers, and data types to detect any changes in the data.

Detection

1.   **Statistical process control**: Use statistical process control methods,such as control charts, to detect changes in the data distribution.
2.   **Drift detection algorithms**: Use algorithms specifically designed fordrift detection, such as the Drift Detection Method (DDM) or the Early Drift Detection Method (EDDM).
3.   **Visual inspection**: Use visual inspection to detect changes in the datadistribution, such as changes in the distribution of features or targets.

Adaptation

1.   **Re-train the model**: Re-train the model on the new data to adapt tothe changed distribution.
2.   **Online learning**: Use online learning methods, such as incrementallearning or streaming learning, to update the model in real-time.
3.   **Ensemble methods**: Use ensemble methods, such as bagging orboosting, to combine the predictions of multiple models and adapt to the changed distribution.
4.   **Transfer learning**: Use transfer learning to adapt a pre-trained modelto the new data distribution.
5.   **Data augmentation**: Use data augmentation techniques to generatenew data that simulates the changed distribution.

Strategies

1.   **Active learning**: Use active learning to select the most informativesamples for labeling and re-training the model.
2.   **Transfer learning**: Use transfer learning to adapt a pre-trained modelto the new data distribution.
3.   **Domain adaptation**: Use domain adaptation techniques to adapt themodel to the new data distribution.
4.   **Meta-learning**: Use meta-learning to learn how to adapt to new datadistributions.

Tools and Techniques

1.   **Data versioning**: Use data versioning tools, such as DVC orPachyderm, to track changes in the data.
2.   **Model versioning**: Use model versioning tools, such as MLflow orTensorFlow, to track changes in the model.
3.   **Drift detection libraries**: Use libraries, such as scikit-learn or PyOD, todetect drift in the data.
4.   **AutoML**: Use automated machine learning (AutoML) tools, such asH2O AutoML or Google AutoML, to automate the process of adapting to data drift.

By following these steps and using these tools and techniques, you can detect and adapt to data drift, ensuring that your machine learning model remains accurate and reliable over time.

Q: how to solve model drift
A: Model drift, also known as concept drift, occurs when the underlying data distribution or relationship between variables changes over time, causing a machine

learning model to become less accurate or even obsolete. To solve model drift, follow these steps:

1. **Monitor model performance**: Regularly track the model's performanceon new, unseen data to detect any changes in accuracy or other key metrics.
2. **Detect drift**: Use statistical methods, such as:
* 　　**Statistical process control**: Monitor the mean and variance of themodel's predictions to detect deviations from the expected behavior.
* 　　**Drift detection methods**: Use techniques like ADWIN, EDDM, orKullback-Leibler divergence to identify changes in the data distribution.
3. **Analyze the cause of drift**: Investigate the reasons behind the drift, such as:
* **Data quality issues**: Changes in data collection, processing, orformatting.
* **Concept drift**: Changes in the underlying relationships betweenvariables.
* **Seasonality or trends**: Periodic or long-term changes in the data.
4. **Re-train or update the model**: Depending on the cause of the drift, consider:
* 　　**Re-training the model**: Use new data to re-train the model, either fromscratch or by fine-tuning the existing model.
* 　　**Updating the model**: Incorporate new data into the existing modelusing techniques like online learning, incremental learning, or transfer learning.
5. **Use adaptive methods**: Implement methods that can adapt to changing data distributions, such as:
* 　　**Online learning**: Update the model in real-time as new data arrives. * **Ensemble methods**: Combine multiple models to improve robustness to drift.
* 　　**Transfer learning**: Use pre-trained models as a starting point andfine-tune them on new data.
6. **Use data augmentation**: Generate new training data by applying transformations to the existing data, such as:
* **Data augmentation techniques**: Apply random transformations (e.g., rotation, scaling, flipping) to increase the diversity of the training data.
7. **Use domain adaptation**: Adapt the model to the new data distribution by:
* **Domain adaptation techniques**: Use methods like adversarial training or multi-task learning to adapt the model to the new data distribution.
8. 　　**Regularly update the training data**: Periodically update the trainingdata to reflect changes in the underlying data distribution.
9. 　　**Use human oversight**: Have human experts review and validate themodel's performance and adapt to changes in the data distribution.
10. 　　**Continuously monitor and evaluate**: Regularly monitor the model'sperformance and re-evaluate the effectiveness of the strategies used to address model drift.

By following these steps, you can detect and address model drift, ensuring that your machine learning models remain accurate and effective over time.

Techniques for handling model drift:
1. **Online learning**: Update the model in real-time as new data arrives.
2. **Incremental learning**: Update the model in batches as new dataarrives.
3. **Transfer learning**: Use pre-trained models as a starting point andfine-tune them on new data.
4. **Ensemble methods**: Combine multiple models to improve robustnessto drift.
5. **Adversarial training**: Train the model to be robust to changes in thedata distribution.
6. **Domain adaptation**: Adapt the model to the new data distribution.
7. **Multi-task learning**: Train the model on multiple tasks to improve itsability to adapt to changes in the data distribution.

Tools and libraries for handling model drift:

1. **scikit-learn**: Provides tools for detecting and addressing model drift.
2. **TensorFlow**: Provides tools for online learning and incrementallearning.
3. **PyTorch**: Provides tools for online learning and incremental learning.
4. **Keras**: Provides tools for online learning and incremental learning.
5. **Amazon SageMaker**: Provides tools for detecting and addressingmodel drift.
6. **Google Cloud AI Platform**: Provides tools for detecting andaddressing model drift.
7. **Microsoft Azure Machine Learning**: Provides tools for detecting andaddressing model drift.

Q: how to make asyncronos call to api

A: Making asynchronous calls to an API allows your application to continue executing other tasks without waiting for the API response. Here are general steps and examples for making asynchronous API calls in various programming languages:

1. JavaScript (Using Fetch API and async/await)

The Fetch API provides an easy, logical way to fetch resources asynchronously across the network. It returns a Promise that resolves to the Response to that request, whether it is successful or not.

```javascript
async function fetchData(url) {
```

```javascript
try {
  const response = await fetch(url);
  if (!response.ok) {
    throw new Error('Network response was not ok');
  }
  const data = await response.json();    console.log(data);
} catch (error) {
  console.error('There has been a problem with your fetch operation:', error);
}}

// Usage
fetchData('https://api.example.com/data');
```

2. Python (Using `requests` and `threading` or `asyncio`)

For asynchronous requests in Python, you can use the `requests` library along with `threading` for simpler cases or `asyncio` for more complex asynchronous operations. However, `requests` itself is synchronous. For truly async operations, consider using `aiohttp`.

Using `threading`:

```python
import requests import
threading

def fetch_data(url):
  response = requests.get(url)   print(response.json())

# Usage
url = 'https://api.example.com/data'
thread = threading.Thread(target=fetch_data, args=(url,))
thread.start()
```

Using `asyncio` and `aiohttp`:

First, install `aiohttp` using pip:
```bash
pip install aiohttp
```

Then, you can make async requests like this:

```python
import aiohttp
import asyncio

async def fetch_data(session, url):
    async with session.get(url) as response:
        data = await response.json()
        print(data)

async def main():
    url = 'https://api.example.com/data'
    async with aiohttp.ClientSession() as session:
        await fetch_data(session, url)

# Usage
asyncio.run(main())
```

3. Java (Using `OkHttp` for Android or Java)

For Android or Java applications, you can use OkHttp for making asynchronous HTTP requests.

First, add OkHttp to your project. If you're using Gradle, add this to your `build.gradle`:

```groovy
implementation 'com.squareup.okhttp3:okhttp:4.10.0'
```

Then, you can make async requests like this:

```java
import okhttp3.OkHttpClient;
import okhttp3.Request;
import okhttp3.Response;

public class MainActivity extends AppCompatActivity {
    private static final String URL = "https://api.example.com/data";

    @Override
```

```java
  protected       void       onCreate(Bundle       savedInstanceState)       {
super.onCreate(savedInstanceState);
  // ...
  OkHttpClient client = new OkHttpClient();
  Request request = new Request.Builder()
    .url(URL)
    .build();

  client.newCall(request).enqueue(new Callback() {
    @Override
    public void onFailure(Call call, IOException e) {       e.printStackTrace();
    }

    @Override
    public void onResponse(Call call, Response response) throws IOException {
      if (response.isSuccessful()) {
        String responseBody = response.body().string();
        // Handle the response body
      }
    }
  });
  }
}
```

4. C# (Using `HttpClient`)

In C#, you can use `HttpClient` for making asynchronous HTTP requests.

```csharp
using       System.Net.Http;       using
System.Threading.Tasks;

public class Program
{
  public static async Task Main(string[] args)
  {
    string url = "https://api.example.com/data";       using
(var client = new HttpClient())
    {
```

```
    HttpResponseMessage      response    =    await    client.GetAsync(url);
response.EnsureSuccessStatusCode();
    string responseBody = await response.Content.ReadAsStringAsync();        //
Handle the response body
  }
 }
}
```
```

These examples illustrate how to make asynchronous calls to an API in different programming languages. The key concept is to use libraries or built-in functionalities that support asynchronous operations, allowing your application to perform other tasks while waiting for the API response.

## Q: how to secure the api

A: Securing an API is crucial to protect sensitive data and prevent unauthorized access. Here are some ways to secure an API:

1. **Authentication**: Implement authentication mechanisms to verify the identity of users or systems making API requests. Common authentication methods include:
* API keys
* OAuth 2.0
* JWT (JSON Web Tokens)
* Basic Auth (username and password)
2. **Authorization**: Control access to API endpoints based on user roles or permissions. This can be done using:  * Role-Based Access Control (RBAC)
* Attribute-Based Access Control (ABAC)
* Mandatory Access Control (MAC)
3. **Encryption**: Use encryption to protect data in transit and at rest:
* HTTPS (TLS/SSL) for encrypting data in transit
* Encrypt sensitive data stored in databases or files
4. **Input Validation**: Validate user input to prevent attacks like SQL injection and cross-site scripting (XSS):
* Use schema validation (e.g., JSON Schema)
* Validate user input against expected formats and ranges
5. **Rate Limiting**: Limit the number of requests from a single IP address or user to prevent brute-force attacks:
* Implement rate limiting using APIs like Redis or Memcached
* Use IP blocking or rate limiting libraries like Fail2Ban
6. **API Gateway**: Use an API gateway to manage API requests and responses:
```

* Handle authentication, rate limiting, and caching
* Provide a single entry point for API requests

7. **Logging and Monitoring**: Log and monitor API requests and responses to detect security issues:
* Use logging libraries like Log4j or Loggly
* Monitor API performance and security using tools like New Relic orDatadog

8. **Secure API Endpoints**: Secure individual API endpoints using:
* HTTP methods (e.g., GET, POST, PUT, DELETE) to restrict access
* API endpoint-specific authentication and authorization

9. **Regular Security Audits**: Perform regular security audits to identify vulnerabilities:
* Use tools like OWASP ZAP or Burp Suite to scan for vulnerabilities
* Conduct manual code reviews and security testing

10. **Keep Dependencies Up-to-Date**: Keep dependencies and libraries up-to-date to ensure you have the latest security patches:
* Use dependency management tools like npm or Maven * Regularly update dependencies and libraries

Additionally, consider implementing:

* **CSRF protection**: Protect against cross-site request forgery attacks
* **CORS**: Implement Cross-Origin Resource Sharing to control access toAPI endpoints from web browsers
* **HSTS**: Implement HTTP Strict Transport Security to enforce HTTPSconnections
* **API documentation**: Provide clear and concise API documentation tohelp users understand API usage and security requirements

Remember, security is an ongoing process. Regularly review and update your API security measures to ensure the protection of your users' data and your system's integrity.

Q: a="aabbcdcfr" get non repeated characters

A: To get non-repeated characters from the string "aabbcdcfr", you can use Python with the following code:

```python
def get_non_repeated_chars(s):
    char_count = {}    for char in s:      if char in char_count:
        char_count[char] += 1      else:
```

```
        char_count[char] = 1

    non_repeated_chars = [char for char, count in char_count.items() if count == 1]

    return non_repeated_chars

a = "aabbcdcfr"
print(get_non_repeated_chars(a))
```

When you run this code with the input "aabbcdcfr", it will output:

```python
['c', 'd', 'f', 'r']
```

This code works as follows:

1. It creates a dictionary `char_count` to store the count of each character in the string.
2. It iterates through the string, incrementing the count for each character in the dictionary.
3. It uses a list comprehension to create a list `non_repeated_chars` of characters that appear only once (i.e., have a count of 1).
4. It returns the list of non-repeated characters.

Q: What is marginal probability?

A: Marginal probability is a concept in probability theory that refers to the probability of a single event or outcome, without considering any other events or outcomes that may be related to it. In other words, it is the probability of an event occurring, regardless of any other events that may have occurred or will occur.

Marginal probability is often denoted by the symbol P(A), where A is the event of interest. For example, if we have a coin toss, the marginal probability of getting heads (P(H)) is 0.5, and the marginal probability of getting tails (P(T)) is also 0.5.

Marginal probability is important in probability theory because it allows us to calculate the probability of an event occurring, without having to consider the joint probability of multiple events. It is also used as a building block for more complex probability calculations, such as conditional probability and joint probability.

To illustrate the concept of marginal probability, consider a simple example:

Suppose we roll a fair six-sided die. The marginal probability of rolling a 6 (P(6)) is 1/6, because there is one favorable outcome (rolling a 6) out of a total of six possible outcomes (1, 2, 3, 4, 5, and 6).

In this example, the marginal probability of rolling a 6 is independent of any other events that may have occurred or will occur. We don't need to consider the probability of rolling a 6 given that we rolled a 3 on the previous roll, or the probability of rolling a 6 given that we will roll a 5 on the next roll. The marginal probability of rolling a 6 is simply 1/6, regardless of any other events.

Marginal probability is a fundamental concept in probability theory, and it has many applications in statistics, engineering, economics, and other fields.

Q: What is conditional probability?

A: Conditional probability is a fundamental concept in probability theory that describes the probability of an event occurring given that another event has already occurred. It is a measure of the probability of an event happening in relation to another event.

The conditional probability of an event A given an event B is denoted as P(A|B) and is read as "the probability of A given B". It represents the probability of A occurring when B has already occurred.

The formula for conditional probability is:

$P(A|B) = P(A ? B) / P(B)$ where:

- P(A|B) is the conditional probability of A given B
- P(A ? B) is the probability of both A and B occurring (the intersection of Aand B)
- P(B) is the probability of B occurring

In other words, conditional probability is a way to update the probability of an event based on new information. It allows us to incorporate the knowledge that another event has occurred, and adjust our probability estimates accordingly.

For example, suppose we want to know the probability that it will rain tomorrow (event A) given that the weather forecast says there is a 70% chance of rain (event B). The conditional probability P(A|B) would represent the probability of it actually raining tomorrow, given that the forecast says it will rain.

Conditional probability has many applications in various fields, including statistics, engineering, economics, and computer science. It is a powerful tool for making informed decisions and predicting outcomes based on available information.

Q: What is Bayes? Theorem and when is it used in data science?

A: **Bayes' Theorem:**

Bayes' Theorem is a fundamental concept in probability theory and statistics, named after Thomas Bayes. It describes the probability of an event based on prior knowledge and new evidence. The theorem is used to update the probability of a hypothesis as more information becomes available.

Mathematical Formula: The Bayes' Theorem formula is:

$$P(H|E) = P(E|H) \ * \ P(H) / P(E)$$

Where:

* $P(H|E)$ is the posterior probability of the hypothesis (H) given the evidence(E)
* $P(E|H)$ is the likelihood of the evidence given the hypothesis
* $P(H)$ is the prior probability of the hypothesis
* $P(E)$ is the prior probability of the evidence

When to Use Bayes' Theorem in Data Science:

Bayes' Theorem is widely used in data science for various applications, including:

1.   **Classification**: Bayes' Theorem is used in Naive Bayes classifiers topredict the class of a new instance based on its features.
2.   **Predictive Modeling**: Bayes' Theorem is used to update the probabilityof a model's parameters based on new data.
3.   **Anomaly Detection**: Bayes' Theorem is used to detect anomalies oroutliers in a dataset by calculating the probability of an instance being an anomaly.
4.   **Recommendation Systems**: Bayes' Theorem is used to recommendproducts or services based on a user's past behavior and preferences.
5.   **Natural Language Processing**: Bayes' Theorem is used in textclassification, sentiment analysis, and language modeling.

Example Use Case:

Suppose we want to predict the probability of a person having a disease based on their symptoms. We have a prior probability of the disease (P(H)) and the likelihood of the symptoms given the disease (P(E|H)). We can use Bayes' Theorem to update the probability of the disease given the symptoms (P(H|E)).

Advantages:

* Bayes' Theorem provides a mathematical framework for updatingprobabilities based on new evidence.
* It allows for the incorporation of prior knowledge and uncertainty in thedecision-making process.
* It is widely used in many fields, including medicine, finance, and socialsciences.

Common Challenges:

* Choosing the right prior distributions for the hypothesis and evidence.
* Dealing with high-dimensional data and complex models.
* Interpreting the results and communicating them to stakeholders.

In summary, Bayes' Theorem is a powerful tool in data science for updating probabilities based on new evidence. It has numerous applications in classification, predictive modeling, anomaly detection, and more. However, it requires careful consideration of prior distributions, model complexity, and interpretation of results.

Q: Define variance and conditional variance.

A: In probability theory and statistics, variance and conditional variance are measures of the spread or dispersion of a random variable.

Variance:
The variance of a random variable X, denoted by Var(X) or σ^2, is a measure of the average distance between the observed values of X and its expected value, E(X). It represents the spread or dispersion of the distribution of X. The variance is calculated as: $Var(X) = E[(X - E(X))^2]$ where E(X) is the expected value of X.

Conditional Variance:
The conditional variance of a random variable X given another random variable Y, denoted by Var(X|Y) or $\sigma^2(X|Y)$, is a measure of the spread or dispersion of X given that Y has taken on a specific value. It represents the average distance between the observed values of X and its conditional expected value, E(X|Y), given that Y has taken

on a specific value. The conditional variance is calculated as: Var(X|Y) = E[(X - E(X|Y))² | Y] where E(X|Y) is the conditional expected value of X given Y.

In other words, the conditional variance measures the variability of X that remains after accounting for the information provided by Y. It is a measure of the uncertainty or unpredictability of X given the knowledge of Y.

For example, in finance, the conditional variance of a stock's returns given the overall market returns can help investors understand the volatility of the stock that is not explained by the overall market.

Q: Explain the concepts of mean, median, mode, and standard deviation.

A: The concepts of mean, median, mode, and standard deviation are fundamental statistical measures used to describe and analyze data. Here's a detailed explanation of each:

1.   **Mean**: The mean, also known as the arithmetic mean, is the averagevalue of a dataset. It's calculated by summing up all the values in the dataset and then dividing by the total number of values. The mean is sensitive to extreme values (outliers) and can be skewed if the data is not normally distributed.

Formula: Mean = (Sum of all values) / (Total number of values)

Example: If the dataset is {1, 2, 3, 4, 5}, the mean is (1 + 2 + 3 + 4 + 5) / 5 = 3.

2.   **Median**: The median is the middle value of a dataset when it'sarranged in ascending or descending order. If the dataset has an even number of values, the median is the average of the two middle values. The median is a better representation of the data than the mean when the data contains outliers or is skewed.

Formula: Median = Middle value (or average of two middle values)

Example: If the dataset is {1, 2, 3, 4, 5}, the median is 3. If the dataset is {1, 2, 3, 4, 5, 6}, the median is (3 + 4) / 2 = 3.5.

3.   **Mode**: The mode is the value that appears most frequently in adataset. A dataset can have multiple modes if there are multiple values that appear with the same frequency. The mode is useful for identifying the most common or typical value in a dataset.

Example: If the dataset is {1, 2, 2, 3, 3, 3}, the mode is 3 because it appears most frequently.

4. **Standard Deviation**: The standard deviation is a measure of thespread or dispersion of a dataset. It represents how much the individual values deviate from the mean. A low standard deviation indicates that the values are close to the mean, while a high standard deviation indicates that the values are spread out.

Formula: Standard Deviation = ?(Sum of (each value - mean)² / (Total number of values - 1))

Example: If the dataset is {1, 2, 3, 4, 5}, the mean is 3, and the standard deviation is approximately 1.41.

In summary:

* Mean: average value of the dataset
* Median: middle value of the dataset
* Mode: most frequent value in the dataset
* Standard Deviation: measure of the spread or dispersion of the dataset

These concepts are essential in statistics and data analysis, and understanding them is crucial for making informed decisions and interpretations of data.

Q: What is the normal distribution and standard normal distribution?

A: The normal distribution and standard normal distribution are two fundamental concepts in statistics.

Normal Distribution:
A normal distribution, also known as a Gaussian distribution or bell curve, is a continuous probability distribution that is symmetric about the mean, showing that data near the mean are more frequent in occurrence than data far from the mean. In a normal distribution, the mean, median, and mode are all equal.

The normal distribution is characterized by the following properties:

1. **Symmetry**: The distribution is symmetric about the mean, meaningthat the left and right sides of the curve are mirror images of each other.
2. **Bell-shaped**: The distribution has a bell-shaped curve, with themajority of the data points clustered around the mean.
3. **Mean, median, and mode**: The mean, median, and mode are allequal in a normal distribution.

The normal distribution is often described by two parameters:

1. **Mean (?)**: The average value of the distribution.
2. **Standard deviation (?)**: A measure of the spread or dispersion of thedistribution.

Standard Normal Distribution:

A standard normal distribution, also known as a z-distribution, is a special case of the normal distribution where the mean (?) is 0 and the standard deviation (?) is 1. This means that the data is standardized to have a mean of 0 and a standard deviation of 1.

The standard normal distribution has the following properties:

1. **Mean**: 0
2. **Standard deviation**: 1
3. **Symmetry**: The distribution is symmetric about the mean (0).
4. **Bell-shaped**: The distribution has a bell-shaped curve, with themajority of the data points clustered around the mean (0).

The standard normal distribution is often used as a reference distribution in statistical analysis, as it provides a common framework for comparing and analyzing data from different distributions. By standardizing data to a z-score, we can compare and analyze data from different distributions using the standard normal distribution.

In summary:

* The normal distribution is a continuous probability distribution that issymmetric about the mean, with a bell-shaped curve.
* The standard normal distribution is a special case of the normaldistribution with a mean of 0 and a standard deviation of 1, used as a reference distribution in statistical analysis.

Q: What is the logistic function (sigmoid function) in logistic regression?

A: The logistic function, also known as the sigmoid function, is a mathematical function used in logistic regression to model the probability of a binary outcome. It's defined as:

Logistic Function (Sigmoid Function):

$?(x) = 1 / (1 + e^{(-x)})$ where:

* $?(x)$ is the logistic function

* x is the input (a linear combination of the predictor variables)* e is the base of the natural logarithm (approximately 2.718)

The logistic function maps any real-valued input x to a value between 0 and 1, which represents the probability of the positive class (e.g., 1) given the input x.

Properties of the Logistic Function:

1.   **S-shaped curve**: The logistic function has an S-shaped curve, whichmeans that it starts at 0, increases gradually, and then levels off at 1.
2.   **Monotonicity**: The logistic function is monotonically increasing,meaning that as x increases, ?(x) also increases.
3.   **Symmetry**: The logistic function is symmetric around the point (0,0.5), meaning that ?(-x) = 1 - ?(x).

Role in Logistic Regression:

In logistic regression, the logistic function is used to model the probability of the positive class (e.g., 1) given the predictor variables. The logistic function is used to transform the linear predictor (a linear combination of the predictor variables) into a probability between 0 and 1.

The logistic regression model can be written as:

$p(y=1|x) = ?(x) = 1 / (1 + e^{(-z)})$ where:

* p(y=1|x) is the probability of the positive class given the input x
* z is the linear predictor (a linear combination of the predictor variables)* ?(x) is the logistic function

The logistic function plays a crucial role in logistic regression, as it allows us to model binary outcomes using a continuous probability distribution.

Q: What is a support vector machine (SVM), and what are its key components?

A: **Support Vector Machine (SVM) Overview**
=====================================

A Support Vector Machine (SVM) is a supervised learning algorithm used for classification and regression tasks. It aims to find the optimal hyperplane that separates the data into different classes with the maximum margin.

Key Components of SVM

----

1.   **Hyperplane**: A hyperplane is a line or plane that separates the datainto different classes. In SVM, the goal is to find the optimal hyperplane that maximizes the margin between classes.

2.   **Margin**: The margin is the distance between the hyperplane and thenearest data points of each class. A larger margin indicates a better separation between classes.

3.   **Support Vectors**: Support vectors are the data points that lie closestto the hyperplane. These points are crucial in defining the position and orientation of the hyperplane.

4.   **Kernel**: A kernel is a mathematical function that maps the originaldata into a higher-dimensional space, where the data becomes linearly separable. Common kernels used in SVM include:

* Linear kernel
* Polynomial kernel
* Radial Basis Function (RBF) kernel
* Sigmoid kernel

5.   **Regularization Parameter (C)**: The regularization parameter controlsthe trade-off between the margin and the misclassification error. A high value of C indicates a stricter penalty for misclassification.

6.   **Decision Function**: The decision function is used to classify new datapoints. It takes the form of a weighted sum of the support vectors, where the weights are determined during training.

How SVM Works

----

1.   **Data Preprocessing**: The data is preprocessed to ensure it is in asuitable format for training.

2.   **Kernel Selection**: A suitable kernel is selected based on the nature ofthe data.

3.   **Model Training**: The SVM model is trained using the preprocesseddata and the selected kernel.

4.   **Hyperplane Optimization**: The optimal hyperplane is found bymaximizing the margin between classes.

5.   **Support Vector Selection**: The support vectors are identified as thedata points that lie closest to the hyperplane.

6.   **Decision Function**: The decision function is used to classify new datapoints.

Advantages and Disadvantages of SVM

Advantages:

* High accuracy in classification tasks
* Robust to noise and outliers* Can handle high-dimensional data

Disadvantages:

* Computationally expensive for large datasets
* Requires careful selection of kernel and regularization parameter* Can be sensitive to overfitting

Real-World Applications of SVM

---

1. **Text Classification**: SVM is widely used in text classification tasks, such as spam detection and sentiment analysis.
2. **Image Classification**: SVM is used in image classification tasks, suchas object recognition and image segmentation.
3. **Biological Data Analysis**: SVM is used in biological data analysis, such as gene expression analysis and protein classification.
4. **Financial Forecasting**: SVM is used in financial forecasting, such asstock market prediction and credit risk assessment.

Q: What is overfitting and how can be overcome this?

A: **Overfitting:**
Overfitting is a common problem in machine learning where a model is too complex and learns the noise in the training data, rather than the underlying patterns. As a result, the model performs well on the training data but poorly on new, unseen data. This occurs when a model is too closely fit to the training data, capturing random fluctuations and outliers rather than the underlying relationships.

Causes of Overfitting:

1. **Model complexity**: Models with too many parameters or layers caneasily overfit the training data.
2. **Insufficient training data**: When the training dataset is small, themodel may not have enough information to generalize well.
3. **Noise in the data**: Noisy or irrelevant features can cause the model tooverfit.

Symptoms of Overfitting:

1. **High training accuracy**: The model performs exceptionally well on thetraining data.
2. **Low test accuracy**: The model performs poorly on new, unseen data.
3. **Large gap between training and test accuracy**: The differencebetween training and test accuracy is significant.

Techniques to Overcome Overfitting:

1. **Regularization**: Add a penalty term to the loss function to discourage large weights.
*   L1 regularization (Lasso regression): adds a term to the loss function thatis proportional to the absolute value of the model's weights.
*   L2 regularization (Ridge regression): adds a term to the loss function thatis proportional to the square of the model's weights.
2.   **Dropout**: Randomly drop out units during training to prevent themodel from relying too heavily on any single unit.
3.   **Early stopping**: Stop training when the model's performance on thevalidation set starts to degrade.
4.   **Data augmentation**: Increase the size of the training dataset byapplying random transformations to the existing data.
5.   **Cross-validation**: Split the data into training and validation sets andevaluate the model's performance on the validation set.
6.   **Simplifying the model**: Reduce the number of parameters or layers inthe model.
7.   **Collecting more data**: Gather more data to increase the size of thetraining dataset.
8.   **Feature selection**: Select a subset of the most relevant features toreduce the dimensionality of the data.
9.   **Batch normalization**: Normalize the input data for each layer toreduce the effect of internal covariate shift.
10.   **Ensemble methods**: Combine the predictions of multiple models toreduce overfitting.

By applying these techniques, you can reduce the likelihood of overfitting and improve the generalization performance of your machine learning models.

Q: Explain the k-nearest neighbors (KNN) algorithm.

A: **K-Nearest Neighbors (KNN) Algorithm**

==

The K-Nearest Neighbors (KNN) algorithm is a supervised learning algorithm used for classification and regression tasks. It is a simple, yet effective algorithm that works by finding the most similar data points (nearest neighbors) to a new, unseen data point.

How KNN Works
----

1.   **Data Collection**: The algorithm starts by collecting a dataset oflabeled examples, where each example is represented by a set of features.
2.   **Distance Calculation**: When a new, unseen data point is presented,the algorithm calculates the distance between the new point and all the existing data points in the dataset.
3.   **K-Nearest Neighbors Selection**: The algorithm selects the k mostsimilar data points (nearest neighbors) to the new point, based on the calculated distances.
4.   **Voting**: For classification tasks, the algorithm assigns the new point tothe class with the most votes among its k-nearest neighbors.
5.   **Regression**: For regression tasks, the algorithm predicts the targetvalue by taking the average of the target values of the k-nearest neighbors.

Key Parameters
----

*   **k**: The number of nearest neighbors to consider. A small value of k canlead to overfitting, while a large value can lead to underfitting.
*   **Distance Metric**: The algorithm uses a distance metric to calculate thesimilarity between data points. Common distance metrics include Euclidean distance, Manhattan distance, and Minkowski distance.

Advantages
----

*   **Simple to Implement**: The KNN algorithm is easy to understand andimplement, making it a great starting point for many machine learning projects.
*   **Flexible**: The algorithm can be used for both classification andregression tasks.
*   **Handling Non-Linear Relationships**: The KNN algorithm can handlenon-linear relationships between features, making it a good choice for datasets with complex relationships.

Disadvantages
----

* **Computational Complexity**: The algorithm can be computationallyexpensive, especially for large datasets.
* **Sensitive to Noise**: The algorithm can be sensitive to noisy data, whichcan affect its performance.
* **Not Suitable for High-Dimensional Data**: The algorithm can suffer fromthe curse of dimensionality, making it less effective for high-dimensional datasets.

Example Use Cases

----

* **Image Classification**: The KNN algorithm can be used for imageclassification tasks, such as classifying images into different categories (e.g., animals, vehicles, buildings).
* **Text Classification**: The algorithm can be used for text classificationtasks, such as spam detection or sentiment analysis.
* **Recommendation Systems**: The KNN algorithm can be used to buildrecommendation systems, such as recommending products or movies based on user preferences.

Code Example

Here is an example of how to implement the KNN algorithm in Python using the scikit-learn library:

```python
from sklearn.neighbors import KNeighborsClassifier from
sklearn.datasets import load_iris
from sklearn.model_selection import train_test_split

# Load the iris dataset iris
= load_iris() X = iris.data y
= iris.target

# Split the dataset into training and testing sets
X_train, X_test, y_train, y_test = train_test_split(X, y, test_size=0.2, random_state=42)

# Create a KNN classifier with k=5
knn = KNeighborsClassifier(n_neighbors=5)
```

```
# Train the model knn.fit(X_train,
y_train)

# Evaluate the model
accuracy = knn.score(X_test, y_test) print("Accuracy:",
accuracy)
```
```

This code example demonstrates how to use the KNN algorithm for classification tasks using the iris dataset. The `KNeighborsClassifier` class is used to create a KNN classifier with k=5, and the `fit` method is used to train the model. The `score` method is then used to evaluate the model's performance on the testing set.

**Q: What is the Naïve Bayes algorithm, what are the different assumptions of Naïve Bayes?**

A: **Naïve Bayes Algorithm:**
The Naïve Bayes algorithm is a family of probabilistic machine learning models based on Bayes' theorem. It is a simple, yet effective, algorithm for classification problems. The goal of the Naïve Bayes algorithm is to predict the class of a new instance based on its features, by calculating the probability of each class given the features.

**Bayes' Theorem:**
The Naïve Bayes algorithm is based on Bayes' theorem, which states that the probability of a class (C) given a set of features (X) is equal to the probability of the features given the class, multiplied by the prior probability of the class, divided by the probability of the features:

$$P(C|X) = P(X|C) \* P(C) / P(X)$$

**Naïve Bayes Assumptions:**
The Naïve Bayes algorithm makes the following assumptions:

1.    **Independence Assumption**: The features are independent of eachother, given the class. This means that the presence or absence of one feature does not affect the presence or absence of another feature.
2.    **Conditional Independence Assumption**: The features are conditionallyindependent of each other, given the class. This means that the probability of a feature given the class is independent of the other features.
3.    **Equal Importance Assumption**: All features are equally important inpredicting the class.
```

4.   **No Correlation Assumption**: The features are not correlated with eachother.

Types of Naïve Bayes:
There are several types of Naïve Bayes algorithms, each with different assumptions:

1.   **Multinomial Naïve Bayes**: Assumes that the features are categoricaland follow a multinomial distribution.
2.   **Bernoulli Naïve Bayes**: Assumes that the features are binary andfollow a Bernoulli distribution.
3.   **Gaussian Naïve Bayes**: Assumes that the features are continuousand follow a Gaussian distribution.
4.   **Complement Naïve Bayes**: A variant of the Multinomial Naïve Bayesalgorithm that is more robust to noise and outliers.

Advantages and Disadvantages:
The Naïve Bayes algorithm has several advantages, including:

* Simple to implement and interpret
* Fast training and prediction times
* Can handle high-dimensional data

However, it also has some disadvantages, including:

* Assumes independence between features, which may not always be true
* Can be sensitive to noise and outliers
* May not perform well on complex datasets with many interactionsbetween features.

Overall, the Naïve Bayes algorithm is a simple and effective algorithm for classification problems, but it may not always be the best choice for complex datasets or datasets with many interactions between features.

Q: Explain the concepts of entropy and information gain in decision trees.

A: Entropy and information gain are fundamental concepts in decision trees, a type of supervised learning algorithm used in machine learning.

Entropy:
Entropy is a measure of the uncertainty or randomness in a dataset. It was first introduced by Claude Shannon in the context of information theory. In the context of decision trees, entropy is used to measure the impurity or uncertainty of a node. A

node with high entropy is considered impure, meaning that the class labels are randomly distributed, while a node with low entropy is considered pure, meaning that the class labels are mostly uniform.

The entropy of a node is calculated using the following formula: H(D) =

- ? (p * log2(p)) where:

* H(D) is the entropy of the node
* p is the proportion of each class label in the node* log2 is the logarithm to the base 2

For example, if a node has two class labels, A and B, with proportions 0.6 and 0.4, respectively, the entropy would be:

H(D) = - (0.6 * log2(0.6) + 0.4 * log2(0.4)) ~= 0.97

Information Gain:

Information gain is a measure of the reduction in entropy or uncertainty that occurs when a node is split using a particular feature or attribute. It is calculated as the difference between the entropy of the parent node and the weighted average entropy of the child nodes.

The information gain is calculated using the following formula: IG(D,

A) = H(D) - ? (|Dj| / |D|) * H(Dj) where:

* IG(D, A) is the information gain of the node
* H(D) is the entropy of the parent node
* Dj is the subset of the data that falls into the j-th child node
* |Dj| is the number of instances in the j-th child node
* |D| is the total number of instances in the parent node
* H(Dj) is the entropy of the j-th child node
For example, if a node has two child nodes, Dj1 and Dj2, with entropies 0.5 and 0.2, respectively, and the parent node has an entropy of 0.97, the information gain would be:

IG(D, A) = 0.97 - (0.6 * 0.5 + 0.4 * 0.2) ~= 0.33

Decision Tree Construction:

Decision trees are constructed by recursively splitting nodes using the feature or attribute that results in the highest information gain. The process continues until a stopping criterion is reached, such as when all instances in a node belong to the same class or when the depth of the tree reaches a maximum.

The decision tree algorithm works as follows:

1. Select the feature or attribute that results in the highest information gain.
2. Split the node using the selected feature or attribute.
3. Recursively apply the algorithm to the child nodes.
4. Stop when a stopping criterion is reached.

By using entropy and information gain, decision trees can effectively identify the most informative features and construct a tree that accurately classifies the data.

Example Use Case:

Suppose we have a dataset of customers with features such as age, income, and credit score, and we want to predict whether they will buy a product or not. We can use a decision tree to classify the customers based on these features.

The decision tree algorithm would work as follows:

1.   Select the feature that results in the highest information gain, say, income.
2.   Split the node using the income feature, say, into two child nodes: highincome and low income.
3.   Recursively apply the algorithm to the child nodes, say, using the agefeature to split the high income node and the credit score feature to split the low income node.
4.   Continue the process until a stopping criterion is reached, such as whenall instances in a node belong to the same class.

The resulting decision tree would provide a clear and interpretable model of the relationships between the features and the target variable, allowing us to make predictions and understand the underlying patterns in the data.

Q: What is the difference between the bagging and boosting model?

A: Bagging and Boosting are two popular ensemble learning techniques used in machine learning to improve the performance and robustness of models. The main difference between them lies in their approach to combining multiple models:

Bagging (Bootstrap Aggregating):

1.   **Random sampling**: Bagging involves creating multiple instances of amodel by training each instance on a random subset of the training data (with replacement).
2.   **Independent models**: Each model is trained independently, and theirpredictions are combined using voting or averaging.
3.   **Reduces overfitting**: Bagging helps reduce overfitting by averagingout the errors of individual models.
4.   **Improves stability**: Bagging improves the stability of the model byreducing the variance of the predictions.

Boosting:

1.   **Sequential training**: Boosting involves training models sequentially,with each subsequent model attempting to correct the errors of the previous model.
2.   **Weighted voting**: Each model is assigned a weight based on itsperformance, and the final prediction is made by weighted voting.
3.   **Focuses on errors**: Boosting focuses on the errors made by theprevious models and tries to correct them.
4.   **Improves accuracy**: Boosting can improve the accuracy of the modelby iteratively refining the predictions.

Key differences:

* **Sampling**: Bagging uses random sampling with replacement, whileBoosting uses the entire training dataset.
* **Model combination**: Bagging combines models using voting oraveraging, while Boosting uses weighted voting.
* **Error correction**: Bagging reduces overfitting by averaging out errors,while Boosting focuses on correcting errors made by previous models. * **Model dependence**: Bagging models are independent, while Boosting models are dependent on each other.

Some popular algorithms that use Bagging include:

* Random Forest
* Bagged Decision Trees

Some popular algorithms that use Boosting include:

* AdaBoost
* Gradient Boosting* XGBoost

In summary, Bagging is a technique that reduces overfitting by averaging out the errors of multiple models, while Boosting is a technique that improves accuracy by iteratively refining the predictions of multiple models.

Q: Describe random forests and their advantages over single-decision trees.

A: **Random Forests: An Ensemble Learning Method**

Random forests are an ensemble learning method that combines multiple decision trees to improve the accuracy and robustness of predictions. This approach was introduced by Breiman in 2001 and has since become a popular and widely-used technique in machine learning.

How Random Forests Work:

1.   **Bootstrap Sampling**: The training data is randomly sampled withreplacement to create multiple subsets, each of which is used to train a separate decision tree.
2.   **Decision Tree Construction**: Each decision tree is constructed using arandom subset of features (attributes) at each node, rather than using all available features.
3.   **Voting**: Each decision tree makes a prediction for a new input, andthe final prediction is made by combining the predictions of all trees, typically through voting (e.g., majority vote).

Advantages over Single-Decision Trees:
1.   **Improved Accuracy**: Random forests can reduce overfitting andimprove the accuracy of predictions by averaging the predictions of multiple trees.
2.   **Reduced Variance**: By combining multiple trees, random forests canreduce the variance of predictions, making them more robust to noise and outliers in the data.
3.   **Handling High-Dimensional Data**: Random forests can handlehigh-dimensional data with a large number of features, as each tree only uses a random subset of features.
4.   **Handling Missing Values**: Random forests can handle missing valuesin the data, as each tree can learn to predict the missing values based on the available features.
5.   **Interpretable   Results**:   Random   forests   provide   feature importancescores, which can be used to understand the contribution of each feature to the predictions.

6.   **Robustness to Overfitting**: Random forests are less prone tooverfitting, as the ensemble approach reduces the impact of individual tree overfitting.

Key Benefits:

1.   **Handling complex interactions**: Random forests can capture complexinteractions between features, which can be difficult to model using single decision trees.
2.   **Handling non-linear relationships**: Random forests can handlenon-linear relationships between features and the target variable.
3.   **Easy to implement**: Random forests are easy to implement andrequire minimal tuning of hyperparameters.

Common Applications:

1.   **Classification**: Random forests are widely used for classificationtasks, such as text classification, image classification, and bioinformatics.
2.   **Regression**: Random forests can be used for regression tasks, suchas predicting continuous outcomes.
3.   **Feature selection**: Random forests can be used for feature selection,as the feature importance scores can be used to select the most relevant features.

In summary, random forests are a powerful ensemble learning method that combines multiple decision trees to improve the accuracy and robustness of predictions. Their advantages over single-decision trees include improved accuracy, reduced variance, and the ability to handle high-dimensional data, missing values, and complex interactions.

Q: What is K-Means, and how will it work?

A: **K-Means Overview** ===============

K-Means is a type of unsupervised machine learning algorithm used for clustering data points into K distinct groups, where K is a predefined number. The algorithm aims to identify patterns or structures in the data by grouping similar data points together.

How K-Means Works

The K-Means algorithm works as follows:

1.   **Initialization**: The algorithm starts by randomly selecting K centroids(also called cluster centers) from the data points.
2.   **Assignment**: Each data point is assigned to the closest centroidbased on the Euclidean distance between the data point and the centroid.
3.   **Update**: The centroids are updated by calculating the mean of all datapoints assigned to each centroid.
4.   **Repeat**: Steps 2 and 3 are repeated until the centroids converge or astopping criterion is met (e.g., a maximum number of iterations).

K-Means Algorithm Steps

Here are the detailed steps of the K-Means algorithm:

Step 1: Initialize Centroids

* Randomly select K data points as the initial centroids.
* Alternatively, use a method like K-Means++ to initialize the centroids.

Step 2: Assign Data Points to Centroids

* Calculate the Euclidean distance between each data point and eachcentroid.
* Assign each data point to the closest centroid based on the minimumdistance.
Step 3: Update Centroids

* For each centroid, calculate the mean of all data points assigned to it.* Update the centroid with the new mean value.

Step 4: Repeat Steps 2 and 3

* Repeat steps 2 and 3 until the centroids converge or a stopping criterion ismet.

Example Use Case

Suppose we have a dataset of customers with their age and income, and we want to segment them into three groups using K-Means. We would:

1. Initialize three centroids randomly.
2. Assign each customer to the closest centroid based on their age andincome.
3. Update the centroids by calculating the mean age and income of eachgroup.

4. Repeat steps 2 and 3 until the centroids converge.

The resulting clusters would represent three distinct customer segments with similar age and income profiles.

Advantages and Disadvantages

Advantages:

* K-Means is a simple and efficient algorithm.
* It can handle large datasets.
* It is widely used in many applications, such as customer segmentation,image compression, and gene expression analysis.

Disadvantages:

* K-Means requires the number of clusters (K) to be predefined.
* It can get stuck in local optima if the initial centroids are not well-chosen.
* It is sensitive to outliers and noise in the data.

Code Example

Here is a simple example of K-Means implemented in Python using scikit-learn:

```python
python import numpy as np
from  sklearn.cluster  import  KMeans  import
matplotlib.pyplot as plt

# Generate sample data
np.random.seed(0) data =
np.random.rand(100, 2)

# Create a KMeans model with K=3 kmeans =
KMeans(n_clusters=3)

# Fit the model to the data kmeans.fit(data)

# Get the cluster labels labels =
kmeans.labels_

# Plot the data with cluster labels plt.scatter(data[:, 0],
data[:, 1], c=labels) plt.show()
```

```
```
```

This code generates random data, creates a K-Means model with K=3, fits the model to the data, and plots the data with cluster labels.

**Q: What is a confusion matrix? Explain with an example.**

A: **Confusion Matrix Overview**
==========================

A confusion matrix is a table used to evaluate the performance of a classification model, such as a machine learning algorithm. It provides a summary of the predictions made by the model against the actual outcomes, allowing for the calculation of various metrics like accuracy, precision, recall, and F1-score.

**Confusion Matrix Structure**
-----------------------------

A typical confusion matrix consists of four cells:

*       **True Positives (TP)**: The number of instances that are correctlypredicted as positive.
*       **False Positives (FP)**: The number of instances that are incorrectlypredicted as positive.
*       **False Negatives (FN)**: The number of instances that are incorrectlypredicted as negative.
*       **True Negatives (TN)**: The number of instances that are correctlypredicted as negative.

**Example: Spam Email Classification**
------------------------------------

Suppose we have a machine learning model that classifies emails as either spam or not spam. We test the model on a dataset of 100 emails, with 60 actual spam emails and 40 actual not spam emails. The model makes the following predictions:

| | Predicted Spam | Predicted Not Spam |
| --- | --- | --- |
| **Actual Spam** | 50 (TP) | 10 (FN) | |
**Actual Not Spam** | 5 (FP) | 35 (TN) |

In this example:

* **True Positives (TP)**: 50 emails that are actually spam and predicted asspam.
```

* **False Positives (FP)**: 5 emails that are actually not spam but predictedas spam.
* **False Negatives (FN)**: 10 emails that are actually spam but predictedas not spam.
* **True Negatives (TN)**: 35 emails that are actually not spam andpredicted as not spam.

Metrics Calculation

Using the confusion matrix, we can calculate various metrics, such as:

* **Accuracy**: (TP + TN) / (TP + TN + FP + FN) = (50 + 35) / 100 = 0.85
* **Precision**: TP / (TP + FP) = 50 / (50 + 5) = 0.91
* **Recall**: TP / (TP + FN) = 50 / (50 + 10) = 0.83
* **F1-score**: 2 * (Precision * Recall) / (Precision + Recall) = 2 * (0.91 *0.83) / (0.91 + 0.83) = 0.87

The confusion matrix provides a clear and concise way to evaluate the performance of a classification model, allowing for the identification of areas for improvement.

Q: Describe the Bernoulli distribution.

A: The Bernoulli distribution is a discrete probability distribution that models a single binary trial or experiment with two possible outcomes: success (1) and failure (0). It is named after the Swiss mathematician Jacob Bernoulli.

In a Bernoulli distribution, the probability of success (1) is denoted by 'p', and the probability of failure (0) is denoted by 'q' or '1-p'. The probability mass function (PMF) of a Bernoulli distribution is given by:

$P(X = 1) = p$ $P(X = 0) = 1 - p$ where X is the random variable representing the outcome of the trial.

The key characteristics of the Bernoulli distribution are:

1. **Binary outcome**: The Bernoulli distribution models a single trial withtwo possible outcomes: success (1) and failure (0).
2. **Fixed probability**: The probability of success (p) is fixed and remainsthe same for each trial.
3. **Independent trials**: Each trial is independent of the others, meaningthat the outcome of one trial does not affect the outcome of another trial.

The Bernoulli distribution is commonly used to model real-world phenomena such as:

* Coin tossing (heads or tails)
* Medical diagnosis (disease present or absent)
* Quality control (defective or non-defective product)* Survey research (yes or no responses)

The Bernoulli distribution is a fundamental building block for more complex probability distributions, such as the binomial distribution, which models the number of successes in a fixed number of independent Bernoulli trials.

Q: What is the binomial distribution?

A: The binomial distribution is a discrete probability distribution that models the number of successes in a fixed number of independent trials, where each trial has a constant probability of success. It is a fundamental concept in statistics and probability theory.

The binomial distribution is characterized by two parameters:

1. **n**: The number of trials (or experiments) conducted.
2. **p**: The probability of success in a single trial.

The binomial distribution gives the probability of obtaining exactly **k** successes in **n** trials, where **k** is an integer between 0 and **n**. The probability of **k** successes is denoted by **P(X = k)**, where **X** is the random variable representing the number of successes.

The probability mass function (PMF) of the binomial distribution is given by:

P(X = k) = (nCk) * (p^k) * (1-p)^(n-k) where:

* **nCk** is the number of combinations of **n** items taken **k** at a time,also written as **C(n, k)** or **"n choose k"**.
* **p^k** is the probability of **k** successes.
* **(1-p)^(n-k)** is the probability of **n-k** failures.

The binomial distribution has several important properties:

* The mean (expected value) of the binomial distribution is **np**.
* The variance of the binomial distribution is **np(1-p)**.
* The binomial distribution is symmetric if **p = 0.5**, and skewed if **p !=0.5**.

The binomial distribution has many applications in statistics, engineering, economics, and other fields, such as:

* Modeling the number of heads in a series of coin tosses.
* Analyzing the number of defects in a manufacturing process.
* Estimating the probability of a certain event occurring in a series ofindependent trials.

Overall, the binomial distribution is a powerful tool for modeling and analyzing binary data, and it has numerous applications in a wide range of fields.

Q: Describe the Poisson distribution and its characteristics.

A: The Poisson distribution is a discrete probability distribution that models the number of events occurring in a fixed interval of time or space, where these events occur with a known constant average rate and independently of the time since the last event. It is commonly used to model the number of times an event happens in a fixed interval of time or space, such as the number of phone calls received by a call center per hour, the number of defects in a manufacturing process, or the number of accidents at a particular intersection per year.

Characteristics of the Poisson Distribution:

1.   **Discrete**: The Poisson distribution is a discrete distribution, meaningthat it can only take on non-negative integer values (0, 1, 2, ...).
2.   **Single Parameter**: The Poisson distribution is characterized by asingle parameter, ? (lambda), which is the average rate of events occurring in the given interval.
3.   **Constant Average Rate**: The average rate of events (?) is constantand does not change over time or space.
4.   **Independence**: The events occur independently of each other,meaning that the occurrence of one event does not affect the probability of another event occurring.
5.   **No Memory**: The Poisson distribution has no memory, meaning thatthe probability of an event occurring does not depend on the time since the last event.
6.   **Non-Negativity**: The Poisson distribution only takes on non-negativeinteger values, which means that the number of events cannot be negative.
7.   **Asymmetry**: The Poisson distribution is asymmetric, with a longer tailto the right, especially for small values of ?.
8.   **Variance**: The variance of the Poisson distribution is equal to themean (?), which means that the spread of the distribution is directly related to the average rate of events.

Key Formulas:

1. **Probability Mass Function (PMF)**: $P(X = k) = (e^{-?}) * (?^k)) / k!$, where k is the number of events, ? is the average rate, and e is the base of the natural logarithm.
2. **Mean**: $E(X) = ?$
3. **Variance**: $Var(X) = ?$

Common Applications:

1. **Quality Control**: Modeling the number of defects in a manufacturingprocess.
2. **Insurance**: Modeling the number of claims received by an insurancecompany.
3. **Telecommunications**: Modeling the number of phone calls receivedby a call center.
4. **Finance**: Modeling the number of transactions in a financial system.
5. **Biology**: Modeling the number of organisms in a population.

Overall, the Poisson distribution is a fundamental probability distribution that is widely used in many fields to model the number of events occurring in a fixed interval of time or space.

Q: Explain the t-distribution and its relationship with the normal distribution.

A: The t-distribution, also known as Student's t-distribution, is a probability distribution that is used to model the distribution of a random variable that follows a normal distribution with unknown population variance. It is a continuous probability distribution that is similar to the normal distribution, but with fatter tails.

Key characteristics of the t-distribution:

1.   **Symmetry**: The t-distribution is symmetric around the mean, just likethe normal distribution.
2.   **Fatter tails**: The t-distribution has fatter tails than the normaldistribution, which means that it is more likely to produce extreme values.
3.   **Degrees of freedom**: The t-distribution is characterized by aparameter called the degrees of freedom (df), which determines the shape of the distribution. The degrees of freedom is related to the sample size and the number of parameters estimated.
4.   **Convergence to normality**: As the degrees of freedom increase, thet-distribution converges to the normal distribution.

Relationship with the normal distribution:

1.   **Limiting case**: The t-distribution converges to the normal distributionas the degrees of freedom approach infinity. In other words, the t-distribution is a generalization of the normal distribution that accounts for the uncertainty in the population variance.

2.   **Similar shape**: The t-distribution has a similar shape to the normaldistribution, with a central peak and declining tails.

3.   **Standardization**: The t-distribution can be standardized to have amean of 0 and a variance of 1, just like the standard normal distribution.

Why use the t-distribution instead of the normal distribution?

1.   **Small sample sizes**: When working with small sample sizes, thet-distribution is a more accurate model for the distribution of the sample mean, as it takes into account the uncertainty in the population variance.

2.   **Unknown population variance**: When the population variance isunknown, the t-distribution is a more conservative and robust choice than the normal distribution, as it accounts for the uncertainty in the variance estimate.

3.   **Statistical inference**: The t-distribution is used in statistical inference,such as hypothesis testing and confidence intervals, when the population variance is unknown or when working with small sample sizes.

Common applications of the t-distribution:

1.   **Hypothesis testing**: The t-distribution is used in hypothesis testing,such as t-tests, to compare the means of two groups or to test the significance of a regression coefficient.

2.   **Confidence intervals**: The t-distribution is used to constructconfidence intervals for the population mean or other parameters.

3.   **Regression analysis**: The t-distribution is used in regression analysisto test the significance of regression coefficients and to construct confidence intervals for the regression line.

In summary, the t-distribution is a probability distribution that is similar to the normal distribution but with fatter tails. It is used to model the distribution of a random variable with unknown population variance and is a more conservative and robust choice than the normal distribution in many statistical applications.

Q: Describe the chi-squared distribution.

A: The chi-squared distribution is a continuous probability distribution that is widely used in statistics, particularly in hypothesis testing and confidence interval construction. It is a special case of the gamma distribution and is often denoted by the symbol ?² (chi-squared).

Definition:

The chi-squared distribution is defined as the sum of the squares of k independent standard normal random variables. In other words, if Z?, Z?, ..., Zk are k independent standard normal random variables (i.e., Z ~ N(0, 1)), then the random variable X = Z?² + Z?² + ... + Zk² follows a chi-squared distribution with k degrees of freedom.

Properties:

1.   **Degrees of freedom:** The chi-squared distribution has one parameter, k, which is called the number of degrees of freedom. The degrees of freedom determine the shape of the distribution.
2.   **Non-negativity:** The chi-squared distribution is defined only for non-negative values, as the sum of squares of real numbers cannot be negative.
3.   **Asymmetry:** The chi-squared distribution is asymmetric, with a long tail to the right.
4.   **Mean and variance:** The mean of the chi-squared distribution is k, and the variance is 2k.

Shapes of the distribution:

The shape of the chi-squared distribution changes as the number of degrees of freedom increases. For:

* k = 1, the distribution is highly skewed to the right.
* k = 2, the distribution is still skewed, but less so than for k = 1.
* k >= 3, the distribution becomes more symmetric and bell-shaped, approaching a normal distribution as k increases.

Applications:

The chi-squared distribution has numerous applications in statistics, including:

1.   **Hypothesis testing:** The chi-squared distribution is used to test hypotheses about categorical data, such as goodness-of-fit tests and tests of independence.

2.   **Confidence intervals:** The chi-squared distribution is used to constructconfidence intervals for parameters, such as the variance of a normal distribution.

3.   **Regression analysis:** The chi-squared distribution is used to test thesignificance of regression coefficients and to construct confidence intervals for regression parameters.

Overall, the chi-squared distribution is a fundamental distribution in statistics, and its properties and applications are widely used in many fields, including social sciences, engineering, and medicine.

Q: What is the difference between z-test, F-test, and t-test?

A: The z-test, F-test, and t-test are all statistical tests used to make inferences about a population based on a sample of data. The main difference between them lies in the type of hypothesis being tested, the distribution of the data, and the assumptions made about the population.

1. **Z-test**:
-       Used for: Testing the mean of a population when the populationstandard deviation is known.
-       Assumptions: The data follows a normal distribution, and the populationstandard deviation is known.
-       Formula: $z = (x̄ - μ) / (σ / \sqrt{n})$, where $x̄$ is the sample mean, $μ$ is thepopulation mean, $σ$ is the population standard deviation, and n is the sample size.
-       Application: Used when the sample size is large (usually > 30) or whenthe population standard deviation is known.

2. **T-test**:
-       Used for: Testing the mean of a population when the populationstandard deviation is unknown.
-       Assumptions: The data follows a normal distribution, and the populationstandard deviation is unknown.
-       Formula: $t = (x̄ - μ) / (s / \sqrt{n})$, where $x̄$ is the sample mean, $μ$ is thepopulation mean, s is the sample standard deviation, and n is the sample size.
-       Application: Used when the sample size is small (usually < 30) or whenthe population standard deviation is unknown.

3. **F-test**:

- Used for: Testing the equality of variances between two or morepopulations.
- Assumptions: The data follows a normal distribution, and the populationshave equal variances (in the case of ANOVA).
- Formula: $F = (s1^2 / ?1^2) / (s2^2 / ?2^2)$, where $s1^2$ and $s2^2$ are thesample variances, and $?1^2$ and $?2^2$ are the population variances.
- Application: Used in analysis of variance (ANOVA) to test the equality ofmeans among multiple groups, and to test the equality of variances between two or more populations.

In summary:
- Use the z-test when the population standard deviation is known and thesample size is large.
- Use the t-test when the population standard deviation is unknown and thesample size is small.
- Use the F-test to compare variances between two or more populations, oras part of ANOVA to compare means among multiple groups.

Q: What is the central limit theorem, and why is it significant in statistics?

A: The central limit theorem (CLT) is a fundamental concept in statistics that describes the behavior of the distribution of sample means as the sample size increases. It states that, given certain conditions, the distribution of sample means will be approximately normally distributed, even if the underlying population distribution is not normal.

Key aspects of the central limit theorem:

1. **Sample size**: The CLT applies to large sample sizes, typically greaterthan 30.
2. **Sample mean**: The theorem focuses on the distribution of samplemeans, rather than individual data points.
3. **Approximate normality**: The distribution of sample means will beapproximately normal, with a mean equal to the population mean (?) and a standard deviation equal to the population standard deviation (?) divided by the square root of the sample size (n).

Why is the central limit theorem significant in statistics?

1. **Simplifies statistical analysis**: The CLT allows us to use normaldistribution-based statistical methods, such as hypothesis testing and

confidence intervals, even when the underlying population distribution is unknown or non-normal.

2.   **Provides a basis for statistical inference**: The CLT is the foundationfor many statistical tests and techniques, including t-tests, ANOVA, and regression analysis.

3.   **Helps to understand the behavior of sample means**: The CLTexplains why sample means tend to be more stable and less variable than individual data points, which is essential for making accurate statistical inferences.

4.   **Enables the use of statistical tables and software**: The CLT is used toconstruct statistical tables, such as the standard normal distribution table (z-table), and is also used in statistical software packages to perform calculations and simulations.

5.   **Has practical applications**: The CLT has numerous practicalapplications in fields such as business, economics, medicine, and social sciences, where it is used to analyze and interpret data, make predictions, and inform decision-making.

Conditions for the central limit theorem to hold:

1.   **Independence**: The data points must be independent and identicallydistributed (i.i.d.).

2.   **Random sampling**: The sample must be randomly selected from thepopulation.

3.   **Large sample size**: The sample size must be sufficiently large(typically greater than 30).

In summary, the central limit theorem is a fundamental concept in statistics that describes the behavior of sample means and provides a basis for statistical inference. Its significance lies in its ability to simplify statistical analysis, provide a basis for statistical inference, and enable the use of statistical tables and software.

Q: Describe the process of hypothesis testing, including null and alternative hypotheses.

A: Hypothesis testing is a statistical process used to make inferences about a population based on a sample of data. The process involves formulating a hypothesis, collecting data, and then testing the hypothesis using statistical methods. The main components of hypothesis testing are the null hypothesis and the alternative hypothesis.

Null Hypothesis (H0):

The null hypothesis is a statement of no effect or no difference. It is a statement of what is expected to happen if there is no real effect or relationship. The null hypothesis is often denoted as H0 and is typically stated in a way that is testable and falsifiable. For example, "There is no significant difference in the average height of men and women." **Alternative Hypothesis (H1 or Ha):**

The alternative hypothesis is a statement of an effect or difference. It is a statement of what is expected to happen if there is a real effect or relationship. The alternative hypothesis is often denoted as H1 or Ha and is typically stated in a way that is testable and falsifiable. For example, "There is a significant difference in the average height of men and women."

Types of Alternative Hypotheses:
There are two types of alternative hypotheses:

1.   **One-tailed alternative hypothesis**: This type of alternative hypothesispredicts a specific direction of the effect. For example, "Men are taller than women on average."
2.   **Two-tailed alternative hypothesis**: This type of alternative hypothesispredicts an effect in either direction. For example, "There is a significant difference in the average height of men and women."

Steps in Hypothesis Testing:

1.   **Formulate the null and alternative hypotheses**: Based on the researchquestion or problem, formulate the null and alternative hypotheses.
2.   **Collect data**: Collect a sample of data that is representative of thepopulation.
3.   **Choose a significance level**: Choose a significance level (?) thatdetermines the maximum probability of rejecting the null hypothesis when it is true.
4.   **Calculate the test statistic**: Calculate a test statistic that measures thedifference between the sample data and the null hypothesis.
5.   **Determine the p-value**: Calculate the p-value, which is the probabilityof observing a test statistic as extreme or more extreme than the one observed, assuming that the null hypothesis is true.
6.   **Make a decision**: Compare the p-value to the significance level (?). Ifthe p-value is less than ?, reject the null hypothesis. Otherwise, fail to reject the null hypothesis.
7.   **Interpret the results**: Interpret the results in the context of theresearch question or problem.

Example:

Suppose we want to test the hypothesis that the average height of men is greater than the average height of women. We collect a sample of 100 men and 100 women and calculate the average height for each group. We then calculate the test statistic and determine the p-value. If the p-value is less than 0.05 ($? = 0.05$), we reject the null hypothesis and conclude that there is a significant difference in the average height of men and women.

Null Hypothesis (H0): $?men = ?women$ (There is no significant difference in the average height of men and women.)

Alternative Hypothesis (H1): $?men > ?women$ (Men are taller than women on average.)

Note: $?men$ and $?women$ represent the population means for men and women, respectively.

Q: What is a p-value in Statistics?

A: In statistics, the p-value (short for probability value) is a measure of the strength of evidence against a null hypothesis. It's a fundamental concept in hypothesis testing and is widely used in various fields, including medicine, social sciences, and engineering.

Definition: The p-value is the probability of observing a result at least as extreme as the one you obtained, assuming that the null hypothesis is true. In other words, it's the probability of getting your results (or more extreme results) by chance, if there is no real effect or relationship.

Interpretation:

*   A small p-value (typically less than 0.05) indicates that the observed resultis unlikely to occur by chance, suggesting that the null hypothesis is likely to be false. This is often referred to as a "statistically significant" result.
*   A large p-value (typically greater than 0.05) indicates that the observedresult is likely to occur by chance, suggesting that the null hypothesis is likely to be true.

Example:

Suppose you want to test whether a new medicine is effective in reducing blood pressure. You collect data from a sample of patients and calculate the average reduction in blood pressure. You then compare this result to a null hypothesis that the medicine has no effect (i.e., the average reduction is zero).

If the p-value is 0.01, this means that there is only a 1% chance of observing the reduction in blood pressure (or a more extreme reduction) if the medicine has no real effect. Since this probability is very low, you can reject the null hypothesis and conclude that the medicine is likely to be effective.

Important notes:

* The p-value is not the probability that the null hypothesis is true or false.
* The p-value is not a measure of the size or importance of the effect.
* The p-value is sensitive to sample size, so a small p-value can beobtained with a large sample size even if the effect is small.

In summary, the p-value is a statistical measure that helps you determine whether the results you obtained are due to chance or if they reflect a real effect or relationship. By interpreting the p-value, you can make informed decisions about whether to reject or accept the null hypothesis.

Q: Explain Type I and Type II errors in hypothesis testing.

A: In hypothesis testing, there are two types of errors that can occur: Type I and Type II errors. These errors occur when the results of a test lead to an incorrect conclusion about the population being studied.

Type I Error:
A Type I error occurs when a true null hypothesis (H0) is rejected in favor of an alternative hypothesis (H1), even though the null hypothesis is actually true. This is also known as a "false positive" error. In other words, a Type I error occurs when we conclude that there is a significant effect or relationship when, in fact, there is none.

Type II Error:
A Type II error occurs when a false null hypothesis (H0) is not rejected in favor of an alternative hypothesis (H1), even though the alternative hypothesis is actually true. This is also known as a "false negative" error. In other words, a Type II error occurs when we fail to detect a significant effect or relationship that actually exists.

To illustrate the difference, consider the following example:

Suppose we want to test whether a new medicine is effective in reducing blood pressure. The null hypothesis (H0) is that the medicine has no effect on blood pressure, while the alternative hypothesis (H1) is that the medicine does reduce blood pressure.

* A Type I error would occur if we conclude that the medicine is effective inreducing blood pressure, when in fact it has no effect.
* A Type II error would occur if we conclude that the medicine has no effecton blood pressure, when in fact it does reduce blood pressure.

The probability of a Type I error is typically denoted by the Greek letter alpha (?), while the probability of a Type II error is denoted by the Greek letter beta (?). The power of a test, which is the probability of correctly rejecting a false null hypothesis, is equal to 1 - ?.

In general, the goal of hypothesis testing is to minimize both Type I and Type II errors. However, it is often impossible to eliminate both types of errors completely, and a trade-off must be made between the two. By adjusting the significance level (?) and the sample size, researchers can balance the risk of Type I and Type II errors and increase the power of the test.

Q: What is the significance level (alpha) in hypothesis testing?

A: The significance level, also known as alpha (?), is a critical concept in hypothesis testing. It represents the maximum probability of rejecting a true null hypothesis, also known as a Type I error.

In simpler terms, the significance level is the threshold beyond which we consider the results of a hypothesis test to be statistically significant. It's a measure of how willing we are to accept the risk of rejecting a true null hypothesis.

Here's how it works:

1. **Null hypothesis (H0)**: A statement of no effect or no difference.
2. **Alternative hypothesis (H1)**: A statement of an effect or difference.
3. **Significance level (?)**: The maximum probability of rejecting H0 whenit is true.

Common values for ? include:

* ? = 0.05 (5%): This is a common choice, meaning that there's a 5%chance of rejecting a true null hypothesis.
* ? = 0.01 (1%): This is a more conservative choice, meaning that there'sonly a 1% chance of rejecting a true null hypothesis.

When we conduct a hypothesis test, we calculate a test statistic and compare it to a critical value or calculate a p-value. If the p-value is less than ?, we reject the null hypothesis and conclude that the results are statistically significant. If the p-value is greater than ?, we fail to reject the null hypothesis, and the results are not statistically significant.

The choice of ? depends on the research question, the field of study, and the potential consequences of a Type I error. A smaller ? (e.g., 0.01) is often used in fields where the consequences of a false positive are severe, such as in medical research. A larger ? (e.g., 0.05) may be used in fields where the consequences of a false positive are less severe, such as in social sciences.

In summary, the significance level (?) is a critical component of hypothesis testing, as it determines the threshold for rejecting a null hypothesis and declaring results statistically significant.

Q: How can you calculate the correlation coefficient between two variables?

A: The correlation coefficient between two variables can be calculated using the following steps:

1.   **Gather the data**: Collect the data for the two variables, X and Y. Thedata should be in the form of pairs (x1, y1), (x2, y2), ..., (xn, yn), where n is the number of observations.

2.   **Calculate the means**: Calculate the means of X and Y, denoted by ?xand ?y, respectively. The mean is calculated by summing up all the values and dividing by the number of observations.

$$?x = (x1 + x2 + ... + xn) / n$$
$$?y = (y1 + y2 + ... + yn) / n$$

3.   **Calculate the deviations**: Calculate the deviations of each data pointfrom the mean for both X and Y.

$$(x1 - ?x), (x2 - ?x), ..., (xn - ?x)$$
$$(y1 - ?y), (y2 - ?y), ..., (yn - ?y)$$

4.   **Calculate the covariance**: Calculate the covariance between X and Y,denoted by cov(X, Y). The covariance is calculated by multiplying the deviations of each data point from the mean for both X and Y, summing them up, and dividing by the number of observations minus 1 (n-1).

cov(X, Y) = ?[(xi - ?x)(yi - ?y)] / (n-1)

5.   **Calculate the variances**: Calculate the variances of X and Y, denotedby ?x^2 and ?y^2, respectively. The variance is calculated by squaring the deviations of each data point from the mean, summing them up, and dividing by the number of observations minus 1 (n-1).

?x^2 = ?(xi - ?x)^2 / (n-1)
?y^2 = ?(yi - ?y)^2 / (n-1)

6.   **Calculate the correlation coefficient**: Calculate the correlationcoefficient, denoted by ? (rho), using the following formula:

? = cov(X, Y) / (?(?x^2) * ?(?y^2))

The correlation coefficient (?) ranges from -1 to 1, where:

* ? = 1 indicates a perfect positive linear relationship between X and Y.
* ? = -1 indicates a perfect negative linear relationship between X and Y.
* ? = 0 indicates no linear relationship between X and Y.
* 0 < ? < 1 indicates a positive linear relationship between X and Y.
* -1 < ? < 0 indicates a negative linear relationship between X and Y.

Note that the correlation coefficient only measures the linear relationship between two variables and does not imply causation.

Q: What is covariance, and how is it related to correlation?

A: Covariance and correlation are two related statistical concepts used to describe the relationship between two variables.

Covariance:
Covariance measures the degree to which two variables change together. It calculates the average of the product of the deviations of two variables from their respective means. The covariance is calculated as:

cov(X, Y) = ?[(xi - ?x)(yi - ?y)] / (n - 1)

where:
- cov(X, Y) is the covariance between variables X and Y
- xi and yi are individual data points
- ?x and ?y are the means of variables X and Y

- n is the number of data points
- ? denotes the sum of the products of the deviations

The covariance can be either positive, negative, or zero. A positive covariance indicates that the variables tend to increase or decrease together. A negative covariance indicates that as one variable increases, the other tends to decrease. A zero covariance suggests that the variables are independent and do not tend to change together.

Correlation:
Correlation, on the other hand, measures the strength and direction of the linear relationship between two variables. It is calculated by standardizing the covariance by dividing it by the product of the standard deviations of the two variables:

corr(X, Y) = cov(X, Y) / (?x * ?y)

where:
- corr(X, Y) is the correlation coefficient between variables X and Y- ?x and
  ?y are the standard deviations of variables X and Y

The correlation coefficient ranges from -1 to 1, where:
- 1 indicates a perfect positive linear relationship
- -1 indicates a perfect negative linear relationship- 0 indicates no linear
  relationship

Relationship between covariance and correlation:
The correlation coefficient is a standardized version of the covariance. By dividing the covariance by the product of the standard deviations, the correlation coefficient provides a more interpretable measure of the relationship between the variables. The correlation coefficient is unitless, whereas the covariance has the same units as the product of the variables.

In summary, covariance measures the degree to which two variables change together, while correlation measures the strength and direction of the linear relationship between two variables. The correlation coefficient is a standardized version of the covariance, providing a more interpretable measure of the relationship between variables.

Q: Explain how to perform a hypothesis test for comparing two population means.

A: Performing a hypothesis test for comparing two population means involves several steps. Here's a step-by-step guide:

Step 1: Define the Null and Alternative Hypotheses

* The null hypothesis (H0) is a statement of no difference between the twopopulation means. It is usually denoted as: H0: ?1 = ?2 (or H0: ?1 - ?2 = 0) * The alternative hypothesis (H1) is a statement of a difference between the two population means. It can be one-tailed (H1: ?1 > ?2 or H1: ?1 < ?2) or two-tailed (H1: ?1 != ?2)

Step 2: Choose a Significance Level (?)

* The significance level (?) is the probability of rejecting the null hypothesiswhen it is true. Common values for ? are 0.05 or 0.01.

Step 3: Collect Sample Data

* Collect two independent random samples from the two populations. Thesamples should be large enough to provide reliable estimates of the population means.
* Calculate the sample means (x?1 and x?2) and sample standarddeviations (s1 and s2) for each sample.

Step 4: Calculate the Test Statistic

* The test statistic is used to determine the likelihood of observing thesample data assuming that the null hypothesis is true.
* The test statistic for comparing two population means is usually thet-statistic: t = (x?1 - x?2) / sqrt((s1^2 / n1) + (s2^2 / n2)) * where n1 and n2 are the sample sizes.

Step 5: Determine the Degrees of Freedom

* The degrees of freedom (df) is the number of independent observationsused to calculate the test statistic.
* For a two-sample t-test, the degrees of freedom is usually calculated as:df = n1 + n2 - 2

Step 6: Look Up the Critical Value or Calculate the P-Value

* Use a t-distribution table or calculator to find the critical value (t-crit) forthe chosen significance level (?) and degrees of freedom (df).
* Alternatively, calculate the p-value using a t-distribution calculator orsoftware. The p-value is the probability of observing a test statistic as extreme or more extreme than the one calculated, assuming that the null hypothesis is true.

Step 7: Make a Decision

* If the p-value is less than the chosen significance level (?), reject the nullhypothesis (H0). This suggests that there is a statistically significant difference between the two population means.
* If the p-value is greater than the chosen significance level (?), fail to rejectthe null hypothesis (H0). This suggests that there is no statistically significant difference between the two population means.

Step 8: Interpret the Results

* If the null hypothesis is rejected, interpret the results in the context of theresearch question or problem.
* If the null hypothesis is not rejected, consider alternative explanations forthe results, such as sampling error or lack of power.

Assumptions

* The hypothesis test for comparing two population means assumes that:
+ The samples are independent and randomly selected from the populations.
+ The samples are normally distributed or approximately normally distributed.
+ The sample sizes are large enough to provide reliable estimates of the population means.
* If these assumptions are not met, alternative tests or transformations maybe necessary.

Q: How do we choose the appropriate kernel function in SVM?

A: Choosing the appropriate kernel function in Support Vector Machines (SVM) is crucial for achieving good performance. The kernel function maps the original data into a higher-dimensional space, allowing for non-linear separation of classes. Here are some steps to help you choose the right kernel function:

1.   **Understand the problem and data**: Before selecting a kernel, it'sessential to understand the nature of your data and the problem you're trying to solve. Consider the dimensionality of the data, the number of features, and the relationships between them.
2.   **Linear kernel**: If your data is linearly separable, a linear kernel (alsoknown as a dot product kernel) is a good choice. This kernel is simple and efficient but may not work well for non-linearly separable data.
3.   **Polynomial kernel**: If your data is not linearly separable, a polynomialkernel can be a good option. This kernel maps the data into a higher-

dimensional space using a polynomial transformation. The degree of the polynomial (e.g., 2, 3, or 4) controls the complexity of the mapping.

4.   **Radial Basis Function (RBF) kernel**: The RBF kernel, also known asthe Gaussian kernel, is a popular choice for many problems. It maps the data into a higher-dimensional space using a Gaussian transformation. The RBF kernel is suitable for non-linearly separable data and can handle high-dimensional data.

5.   **Sigmoid kernel**: The sigmoid kernel is similar to the RBF kernel butuses a sigmoid transformation instead. It's less commonly used than the RBF kernel but can be effective in certain situations.

6.   **Other kernels**: There are many other kernel functions available, suchas the Laplace kernel, the exponential kernel, and the wavelet kernel. These kernels are often used for specific problem domains or data types (e.g., image or text data).

7.   **Kernel selection criteria**: When choosing a kernel, consider thefollowing criteria:

*   **Computational complexity**: Some kernels, like the RBF kernel, can becomputationally expensive. Choose a kernel that balances accuracy and computational efficiency.

*   **Overfitting**: Avoid kernels that are too complex or have too manyparameters, as they can lead to overfitting.

*   **Interpretability**: Consider the interpretability of the kernel. Forexample, the linear kernel is easy to interpret, while the RBF kernel can be more difficult to understand.

8.   **Cross-validation**: Use cross-validation to evaluate the performance ofdifferent kernels on your dataset. This will help you choose the best kernel for your specific problem.

9.   **Hyperparameter tuning**: Once you've selected a kernel, tune itshyperparameters (e.g., the degree of the polynomial kernel or the width of the RBF kernel) to optimize performance.

Some popular kernel selection strategies include:

*   **Grid search**: Try a range of kernel functions and hyperparameters, andselect the best combination based on cross-validation performance.

*   **Random search**: Randomly sample kernel functions and hyperparameters, and select the best combination based on cross-validation performance.

*   **Bayesian optimization**: Use Bayesian optimization techniques tosearch for the optimal kernel function and hyperparameters.

Ultimately, the choice of kernel function depends on the specific characteristics of your dataset and the problem you're trying to solve. Experimenting with different kernels and evaluating their performance using cross-validation is the best way to determine the most suitable kernel for your SVM model.

Q: How does Naïve Bayes handle categorical and continuous features?

A: Naïve Bayes is a family of probabilistic machine learning models that are based on Bayes' theorem. It can handle both categorical and continuous features, but it does so in different ways.

Categorical Features:

For categorical features, Naïve Bayes uses a multinomial distribution to model the probability of each category. The probability of a feature being in a particular category is calculated as the frequency of that category in the training data. The model assumes that the features are conditionally independent, given the class label.

For example, if we have a categorical feature "color" with categories "red", "blue", and "green", the model would calculate the probability of each category as follows:

P(color="red" | class="positive") = Number of "red" instances in the positive class / Total number of instances in the positive class

Continuous Features:

For continuous features, Naïve Bayes uses a Gaussian distribution (also known as a normal distribution) to model the probability of each feature. The Gaussian distribution is characterized by a mean and standard deviation, which are calculated from the training data.

The probability of a feature value is calculated as follows:

P(feature | class) = (1 / sqrt(2 * pi * sigma^2)) * exp(-((feature - mu)^2) / (2 * sigma^2))
where mu is the mean, sigma is the standard deviation, and feature is the value of the feature.

The model assumes that the features are conditionally independent, given the class label, and that the features follow a Gaussian distribution.

Types of Naïve Bayes:

There are several types of Naïve Bayes models, including:

* Multinomial Naïve Bayes: used for categorical features
* Gaussian Naïve Bayes: used for continuous features* Bernoulli Naïve Bayes: used for binary features

Each type of Naïve Bayes model is suitable for different types of data and features.

Assumptions:

Naïve Bayes makes several assumptions about the data, including:

* Conditional independence: the features are independent, given the classlabel
* Gaussian distribution: the continuous features follow a Gaussiandistribution
* Multinomial distribution: the categorical features follow a multinomialdistribution

If these assumptions are not met, the model may not perform well. However, Naïve Bayes is often robust to violations of these assumptions and can still perform well in many cases.

Q: What are imbalanced datasets and how can we handle them?

A: Imbalanced datasets are datasets where the number of instances in one or more classes significantly outweighs the number of instances in other classes. This can lead to biased models that perform well on the majority class but poorly on the minority class. Handling imbalanced datasets is crucial to ensure that the models are fair and accurate.

Types of Imbalance:

1.   **Class imbalance**: One class has a significantly larger number ofinstances than the other classes.
2.   **Instance imbalance**: Some instances have a much higher weight orimportance than others.
3.   **Feature imbalance**: Some features have a much larger range orvariance than others.

Effects of Imbalance:

1.   **Biased models**: Models may become biased towards the majorityclass, resulting in poor performance on the minority class.
2.   **Poor generalization**: Models may not generalize well to new, unseendata, especially if the minority class is underrepresented.

3. **Overfitting**: Models may overfit to the majority class, resulting in poorperformance on the minority class.

Techniques to Handle Imbalance:

1. **Oversampling the minority class**: Creating additional instances of theminority class to balance the dataset.
2. **Undersampling the majority class**: Reducing the number of instancesin the majority class to balance the dataset.
3. **SMOTE (Synthetic Minority Over-sampling Technique)**: Creatingsynthetic instances of the minority class to balance the dataset.
4. **ADASYN (Adaptive Synthetic Sampling)**: Creating synthetic instancesof the minority class based on the density of the minority class.
5. **Cost-sensitive learning**: Assigning different costs to different classesto penalize misclassifications of the minority class.
6. **Ensemble methods**: Combining multiple models to improveperformance on the minority class.
7. **Anomaly detection**: Treating the minority class as anomalies andusing specialized algorithms to detect them.
8. **Data augmentation**: Generating new instances of the minority classthrough data augmentation techniques, such as rotation, scaling, and flipping.
9. **Transfer learning**: Using pre-trained models and fine-tuning them onthe imbalanced dataset.
10. **Class weighting**: Assigning different weights to different classes topenalize misclassifications of the minority class.

Best Practices:

1. **Evaluate models on multiple metrics**: Use metrics such as precision,recall, F1-score, and AUC-ROC to evaluate model performance on both classes.
2. **Use class weights or cost-sensitive learning**: Assign different costs orweights to different classes to penalize misclassifications of the minority class.
3. **Monitor performance on the minority class**: Regularly monitor modelperformance on the minority class to detect any degradation in performance.
4. **Collect more data**: If possible, collect more data to balance thedataset and reduce the impact of imbalance.

By understanding the types of imbalance, their effects, and the techniques to handle them, you can develop more accurate and fair models that perform well on all classes, even in the presence of imbalance.

Q: What are outliers in the dataset and how can we detect and remove them?

A: Outliers in a dataset are data points that are significantly different from the other observations. They can be extremely high or low values that don't fit the pattern of the rest of the data. Outliers can be due to various reasons such as:

1. **Measurement errors**: Incorrect or imprecise measurements can leadto outliers.
2. **Data entry errors**: Typos or incorrect data entry can result in outliers.
3. **Sampling errors**: Sampling biases or errors can lead to outliers.
4. **Natural variability**: In some cases, outliers can be a natural part of thedata distribution.

Detecting and removing outliers is essential because they can:

1. **Affect statistical analysis**: Outliers can significantly impact statisticalmodels, leading to incorrect conclusions.
2. **Skew data distribution**: Outliers can alter the shape of the datadistribution, making it difficult to model or analyze.
3. **Influence machine learning models**: Outliers can affect theperformance of machine learning models, leading to poor predictions or classifications.

Methods to detect outliers:

1. **Visual inspection**: Plotting the data using histograms, box plots, orscatter plots can help identify outliers.
2. **Statistical methods**: Using statistical measures such as mean,median, and standard deviation to identify data points that are more than 2-3 standard deviations away from the mean.
3. **Z-score method**: Calculating the z-score for each data point, whichmeasures the number of standard deviations from the mean. Data points with a z-score greater than 2-3 are considered outliers.
4. **Modified Z-score method**: A variation of the z-score method that ismore robust to non-normal data distributions.
5. **Density-based methods**: Using density-based methods such asDBSCAN (Density-Based Spatial Clustering of Applications with Noise) to identify outliers.

Methods to remove outliers:

1. **Deleting outliers**: Simply removing the outlier data points from thedataset.

2.   **Winsorization**: Replacing outliers with a value closer to the median ormean, such as the 5th or 95th percentile.
3.   **Truncation**: Truncating the data at a certain percentile, such as the1st or 99th percentile.
4.   **Transforming data**: Transforming the data using techniques such aslogarithmic or square root transformations to reduce the effect of outliers.
5.   **Using robust statistical methods**: Using statistical methods that arerobust to outliers, such as the median or interquartile range.

Important considerations:

1.   **Understand the context**: Before removing outliers, understand thecontext of the data and the potential reasons for the outliers.
2.   **Evaluate the impact**: Evaluate the impact of removing outliers on thestatistical analysis or machine learning models.
3.   **Document the process**: Document the process of detecting andremoving outliers, including the methods used and the criteria for removal.

In summary, outliers can significantly impact statistical analysis and machine learning models. Detecting and removing outliers requires a combination of visual inspection, statistical methods, and careful consideration of the context and potential impact.

Q: What is the curse of dimensionality And How can we overcome this?

A: **The Curse of Dimensionality**
The curse of dimensionality is a phenomenon in data analysis and machine learning where the number of dimensions or features in a dataset increases exponentially, leading to a decrease in the accuracy and performance of models. This curse was first identified by Richard Bellman in 1957 and has since become a fundamental challenge in data science.

As the number of dimensions increases, the following issues arise:

1.   **Data becomes sparse**: With more dimensions, the data becomesincreasingly sparse, making it difficult to find meaningful patterns and relationships.
2.   **Noise and irrelevant features**: High-dimensional data often includesnoise and irrelevant features, which can negatively impact model performance.
3.   **Overfitting**: Models may become overly complex and prone tooverfitting, which reduces their ability to generalize to new, unseen data.

4.   **Computational   complexity**:   High-dimensional   data   requires morecomputational resources and time to process, making it challenging to analyze and visualize.

Consequences of the Curse of Dimensionality

The curse of dimensionality has several consequences, including:

1.   **Decreased   model   accuracy**:   As   the   number   of   dimensions increases,model accuracy often decreases.
2.   **Increased risk of overfitting**: High-dimensional data increases the riskof overfitting, which can lead to poor model performance on new data.
3.   **Reduced interpretability**: High-dimensional data can make itchallenging to interpret the results and understand the relationships between variables.

Overcoming the Curse of Dimensionality

To overcome the curse of dimensionality, several techniques can be employed:

1. **Dimensionality reduction**: Reduce the number of dimensions using techniques such as:
* Principal Component Analysis (PCA)
* t-Distributed Stochastic Neighbor Embedding (t-SNE) * Autoencoders
* Feature selection
2.   **Feature   engineering**:   Create   new   features   that   are   relevant andinformative, and eliminate irrelevant features.
3.   **Regularization techniques**: Use regularization techniques, such as: * L1 and L2 regularization
* Dropout
* Early stopping
4.   **Ensemble   methods**:   Combine   multiple   models   to   improve overallperformance and reduce the impact of the curse of dimensionality.
5.   **Non-linear dimensionality reduction**: Use non-linear techniques, suchas:
* Kernel PCA
* Isomap
* Locally Linear Embedding (LLE)
6.   **Data   preprocessing**:   Preprocess   the   data   to   remove   noise, handlemissing values, and normalize the features.
7.   **Model   selection**:   Choose   models   that   are   robust   to   high-dimensionaldata, such as: * Random forests
* Gradient boosting

* Support vector machines (SVMs)

By applying these techniques, data scientists and machine learning practitioners can mitigate the effects of the curse of dimensionality and develop more accurate and robust models.

Q: How does the random forest algorithm handle feature selection?

A: The random forest algorithm handles feature selection in several ways:

1.   **Random Feature Selection**: During the construction of each decisiontree, a random subset of features is selected at each node. This process is known as "feature bagging" or "attribute bagging". The number of features to consider at each node is a hyperparameter that can be tuned.
2.   **Gini Importance**: After training, the random forest algorithm calculatesthe importance of each feature using the Gini importance measure. The Gini importance is a measure of how much each feature contributes to the reduction of impurity (e.g., Gini index or entropy) in the data. Features with higher Gini importance are considered more important for the model.
3.   **Permutation Importance**: Another way to evaluate feature importanceis through permutation importance. This method involves randomly permuting the values of a feature and measuring the decrease in model performance. Features with a larger decrease in performance are considered more important.
4.   **Recursive Feature Elimination (RFE)**: Random forest can be used asa feature selector in conjunction with recursive feature elimination. RFE works by recursively removing the least important features until a specified number of features is reached.
5.   **Embedded Feature Selection**: Random forest can be used as anembedded feature selection method, where the feature selection is performed as part of the model training process. The model learns to select the most relevant features during training.

The advantages of using random forest for feature selection are:

*   **Handling high-dimensional data**: Random forest can handlehigh-dimensional data with a large number of features.
*   **Handling correlated features**: Random forest can handle correlatedfeatures by selecting a subset of features that are most relevant for the model.
*   **Robustness to noise**: Random forest is robust to noisy or irrelevantfeatures, as the model can learn to ignore them.

However, the limitations of using random forest for feature selection are:

* **Computational cost**: Calculating feature importance can becomputationally expensive, especially for large datasets.
* **Interpretability**: The feature importance scores can be difficult tointerpret, especially when there are many features.

Overall, random forest is a powerful algorithm for feature selection, and its ability to handle high-dimensional data and correlated features makes it a popular choice in many applications.

Q: What is feature engineering? Explain the different feature engineering methods.

A: Feature engineering is the process of selecting and transforming raw data into features that are more suitable for modeling. It involves using domain knowledge and statistical techniques to create new features from existing ones, with the goal of improving the performance of a machine learning model. Feature engineering is a crucial step in the machine learning pipeline, as it can significantly impact the accuracy and robustness of the model.

There are several feature engineering methods, which can be categorized into the following:

1. **Data Transformation**: This involves transforming existing features into new ones using mathematical functions, such as:
* Log transformation: to reduce the effect of outliers and skewness.
* Standardization: to scale features to a common range.
* Normalization: to scale features to a common range, usually between 0and 1.
2. **Feature Extraction**: This involves extracting new features from existing ones, such as:
* Principal Component Analysis (PCA): to reduce dimensionality andextract relevant features.
* t-Distributed Stochastic Neighbor Embedding (t-SNE): to reducedimensionality and visualize high-dimensional data.
* Feature selection: to select a subset of the most relevant features.
3. **Feature Construction**: This involves creating new features from existing ones, such as:
* Polynomial features: to create new features by combining existing onesusing polynomial equations.
* Interaction features: to create new features by combining existing onesusing interaction terms.
* Fourier transform: to extract frequency features from time-series data.

4. **Encoding**: This involves converting categorical features into numerical features, such as:

* One-hot encoding: to convert categorical features into binary vectors.
* Label encoding: to convert categorical features into numerical values.
* Binary encoding: to convert categorical features into binary vectors.

5. **Handling Missing Values**: This involves imputing missing values in the data, such as:

* Mean imputation: to replace missing values with the mean of the feature. * Median imputation: to replace missing values with the median of the feature.
* Imputation using regression: to replace missing values using a regressionmodel.

6. **Text Feature Engineering**: This involves extracting features from text data, such as:

* Bag-of-words: to represent text data as a vector of word frequencies.
* Term Frequency-Inverse Document Frequency (TF-IDF): to representtext data as a vector of word importance.
* Word embeddings: to represent words as vectors in a high-dimensionalspace.

7. **Time-Series Feature Engineering**: This involves extracting features from time-series data, such as:

* Time-domain features: to extract features from the time-domainrepresentation of the data.
* Frequency-domain features: to extract features from the frequency-domain representation of the data.
* Seasonal decomposition: to extract seasonal and trend components fromthe data.

8. **Domain-Specific Feature Engineering**: This involves using domain knowledge to create features that are specific to the problem domain, such as:

* Creating features based on business rules or expert knowledge. * Using domain-specific libraries or tools to extract features.

These are some of the common feature engineering methods used in machine learning. The choice of method depends on the specific problem, data, and model being used.

Q: What is DBSCAN and How we will use it?

A: **DBSCAN Overview** ================

DBSCAN (Density-Based Spatial Clustering of Applications with Noise) is a popular unsupervised machine learning algorithm used for clustering data points based on their density and proximity to each other. It was introduced in 1996 by Martin Ester, Hans-Peter Kriegel, Jörg Sander, and Xiaowei Xu.

How DBSCAN Works

DBSCAN works by identifying clusters of high density and separating them from noise (data points that don't belong to any cluster). The algorithm uses two main parameters:

1. **? (Epsilon)**: The maximum distance between two points in a cluster.
2. **MinPts**: The minimum number of points required to form a denseregion.

Here's a step-by-step explanation of the DBSCAN algorithm:

1. **Initialization**: Choose an arbitrary data point and mark it as visited.
2. **Find Neighbors**: Find all points within a distance of ? from the chosenpoint.
3. **Check Density**: If the number of neighbors is greater than or equal toMinPts, the point is a core point.
4. **Expand Cluster**: If the point is a core point, expand the cluster byadding all neighboring points that are also core points.
5. **Label Points**: Label all points in the cluster as belonging to the samecluster.
6. **Repeat**: Repeat the process for all unvisited points.

Types of Points in DBSCAN

DBSCAN categorizes points into three types:

1. **Core Points**: Points with at least MinPts neighbors within a distanceof ?.
2. **Border Points**: Points that are not core points but are within adistance of ? from a core point.
3. **Noise Points**: Points that are neither core points nor border points.

Example Use Cases

DBSCAN has numerous applications in various fields, including:

1. **Geographic Information Systems (GIS)**: Clustering geographiclocations based on density.

2. **Network Analysis**: Identifying clusters of nodes in a network.
3. **Image Segmentation**: Segmenting images based on density andproximity.
4. **Customer Segmentation**: Clustering customers based on theirbehavior and demographics.

Code Example (Python)

Here's an example of using DBSCAN in Python with the scikit-learn library:

```python
import numpy as np
from sklearn.cluster import DBSCAN import matplotlib.pyplot as plt

# Generate sample data np.random.seed(0)
data = np.random.rand(100, 2)

# Create a DBSCAN object
dbscan = DBSCAN(eps=0.3, min_samples=10)

# Fit the data dbscan.fit(data)

# Get the cluster labels labels =
dbscan.labels_

# Plot the clusters
plt.scatter(data[:, 0], data[:, 1], c=labels) plt.show()
```

This code generates random data, applies DBSCAN with ? = 0.3 and MinPts = 10, and plots the resulting clusters.

Advantages and Disadvantages

Advantages:

* DBSCAN can handle noise and outliers effectively.
* It can identify clusters of varying densities.* It's robust to the choice of parameters.

Disadvantages:

* DBSCAN can be sensitive to the choice of ? and MinPts.

* It may not perform well with high-dimensional data.

* It can be computationally expensive for large datasets.

In conclusion, DBSCAN is a powerful clustering algorithm that can effectively identify clusters of varying densities and handle noise and outliers. However, it requires careful tuning of parameters and can be computationally expensive for large datasets.

Q: Explain the concept of silhouette score in clustering evaluation.

A: The Silhouette Score is a measure used to evaluate the quality of clustering in unsupervised learning. It was first introduced by Peter J. Rousseeuw in 1987. The score ranges from -1 to 1, where:

- A high value (close to 1) indicates that the object is well matched to itsown cluster and poorly matched to neighboring clusters.
- A low value (close to -1) indicates that the object has been assigned to thewrong cluster, as a different cluster is more similar.
- A value close to 0 indicates that the object is on or very close to the borderbetween two neighboring clusters.

The Silhouette Score is calculated for each data point using the following formula:

$$**s(i) = (b(i) - a(i)) / max(a(i), b(i))**$$

where:
- **$s(i)$** is the Silhouette Score for the i-th data point.
- **$a(i)$** is the average distance from the i-th data point to all other points inthe same cluster (intra-cluster distance).
- **$b(i)$** is the average distance from the i-th data point to all points in thenearest neighboring cluster (inter-cluster distance).

The overall Silhouette Score for a clustering model is the mean of the Silhouette Scores for all data points.

Here's how to interpret the Silhouette Score:

* **Silhouette Score > 0.5**: The clustering model is doing well, and the data points are well-separated and assigned to the correct clusters. * **Silhouette Score between 0 and 0.5**: The clustering model is doing reasonably well, but there might be some overlap between clusters. * **Silhouette Score < 0**: The clustering model is not doing well, and the data points are not well-separated or are assigned to the wrong clusters.

The Silhouette Score is useful for evaluating the quality of clustering models, especially when the number of clusters is not known in advance. However, it can be computationally expensive for large datasets and may not work well with clusters of varying densities.

Q: What is the relationship between eigenvalues and eigenvectors in PCA?

A: In Principal Component Analysis (PCA), eigenvalues and eigenvectors are closely related and play a crucial role in the dimensionality reduction process.

Eigenvalues:
In PCA, eigenvalues represent the amount of variance explained by each principal component. They are scalar values that measure the spread or dispersion of the data along each principal axis. The eigenvalues are calculated from the covariance matrix of the data and are arranged in descending order. The first eigenvalue corresponds to the first principal component, which explains the most variance in the data. The second eigenvalue corresponds to the second principal component, which explains the second most variance, and so on.

Eigenvectors:
Eigenvectors, on the other hand, represent the directions of the new axes (principal components) in the transformed space. They are vectors that define the orientation of the new axes and are used to project the original data onto the new axes. Each eigenvector is associated with an eigenvalue, and the eigenvector corresponding to the largest eigenvalue is the first principal component.

Relationship between eigenvalues and eigenvectors:
The relationship between eigenvalues and eigenvectors in PCA is as follows:

1.   **Eigenvalue magnitude:** The magnitude of an eigenvalue representsthe amount of variance explained by the corresponding eigenvector (principal component). A larger eigenvalue indicates that the corresponding eigenvector explains more variance in the data.
2.   **Eigenvector direction:** The direction of an eigenvector represents thedirection of the new axis (principal component) in the transformed space. The eigenvector corresponding to the largest eigenvalue is the first principal component, which explains the most variance in the data.

3.   **Orthogonality:** Eigenvectors are orthogonal to each other, meaningthat they are perpendicular and do not overlap. This ensures that each principal component explains a unique aspect of the data.

4.   **Ranking:** The eigenvalues and eigenvectors are ranked indescending order of the eigenvalues. This means that the first eigenvector (first principal component) explains the most variance, the second eigenvector explains the second most variance, and so on.

In summary, eigenvalues and eigenvectors are fundamental concepts in PCA, and their relationship is essential for understanding the dimensionality reduction process. Eigenvalues represent the amount of variance explained by each principal component, while eigenvectors represent the directions of the new axes in the transformed space. The relationship between eigenvalues and eigenvectors allows us to identify the most important features in the data and to reduce the dimensionality of the data while retaining most of the information.

Q: What are the ROC and AUC, explain its significance in binary classification.

A: **ROC and AUC: Understanding their Significance in Binary Classification**

==
===========

In binary classification, the Receiver Operating Characteristic (ROC) curve and the Area Under the Curve (AUC) are essential metrics used to evaluate the performance of a model. In this explanation, we will delve into the concepts of ROC and AUC, their significance, and how they are used in binary classification.

What is the ROC Curve?

The ROC curve is a graphical representation of a model's ability to distinguish between two classes (positive and negative) at different thresholds. It plots the True Positive Rate (TPR) against the False Positive Rate (FPR) at various thresholds.

*   **True Positive Rate (TPR)**: The proportion of actual positive instancesthat are correctly predicted as positive.

*   **False Positive Rate (FPR)**: The proportion of actual negativeinstances that are incorrectly predicted as positive.

The ROC curve provides a visual representation of the trade-off between TPR and FPR. A good model will have a curve that is closer to the top-left corner, indicating a high TPR and a low FPR.

What is the AUC?

The Area Under the Curve (AUC) is a summary metric that represents the entire ROC curve. It measures the model's ability to distinguish between positive and negative classes. The AUC value ranges from 0 to 1, where:
*   **AUC = 1**: Perfect classification (no overlap between positive andnegative classes)
*   **AUC = 0.5**: Random classification (no better than chance)*   **AUC < 0.5**: Worse than random classification

Significance of ROC and AUC in Binary Classification

The ROC curve and AUC are significant in binary classification because they:

1.   **Evaluate Model Performance**: The ROC curve and AUC provide acomprehensive evaluation of a model's performance, considering both TPR and FPR.
2.   **Compare Models**: The AUC value allows for comparison betweendifferent models, making it easier to choose the best-performing model.
3.   **Identify Optimal Thresholds**: The ROC curve helps identify theoptimal threshold for classification, balancing TPR and FPR.
4.   **Handle Class Imbalance**: The AUC is a useful metric for evaluatingmodels on imbalanced datasets, where the number of positive and negative instances is significantly different.

Example Use Case

Suppose we have a binary classification model that predicts whether a customer will churn (positive class) or not (negative class). We can use the ROC curve and AUC to evaluate the model's performance.

Threshold	TPR	FPR
0.3	0.8	0.2
0.4	0.7	0.1

| 0.5 | 0.6 | 0.05 |

By plotting the ROC curve, we can visualize the trade-off between TPR and FPR. The AUC value can be calculated to provide a summary metric of the model's performance.

Code Example

Here's an example code snippet in Python using scikit-learn to calculate the ROC curve and AUC:

```python
from sklearn.metrics import roc_curve, auc from
sklearn.model_selection import train_test_split from
sklearn.linear_model import LogisticRegression import
numpy as np

# Generate sample data
np.random.seed(0) X =
np.random.rand(100, 2) y =
np.random.randint(0, 2, 100)

# Split data into training and testing sets
X_train,    X_test,   y_train,   y_test   =   train_test_split(X,   y,   test_size=0.2,
random_state=42)

# Train a logistic regression model model =
LogisticRegression() model.fit(X_train,
y_train)

# Predict probabilities
y_pred_proba = model.predict_proba(X_test)[:, 1]

# Calculate ROC curve and AUC
fpr, tpr, thresholds = roc_curve(y_test, y_pred_proba) auc_value =
auc(fpr, tpr)

print("AUC:", auc_value)
```

In this example, we train a logistic regression model on a sample dataset and calculate the ROC curve and AUC using the `roc_curve` and `auc` functions from scikit-learn.

In conclusion, the ROC curve and AUC are essential metrics in binary classification, providing a comprehensive evaluation of a model's performance and helping to identify optimal thresholds and compare models.

Q: Describe batch gradient descent, stochastic gradient descent, and mini-batch gradient descent.

A: Batch Gradient Descent, Stochastic Gradient Descent, and Mini-Batch Gradient Descent are three variants of Gradient Descent, a popular optimization algorithm used in machine learning to minimize the loss function of a model.

Batch Gradient Descent (BGD)
Batch Gradient Descent is the most basic form of Gradient Descent. It works by considering the entire dataset at once to compute the gradient of the loss function. Here's a step-by-step overview of BGD:

1.   **Compute the gradient**: Calculate the gradient of the loss function withrespect to the model's parameters using the entire dataset.
2.   **Update the parameters**: Update the model's parameters bysubtracting the product of the learning rate and the computed gradient.
3.   **Repeat**: Repeat steps 1 and 2 until convergence or a stoppingcriterion is reached.

The advantages of BGD are:
*   **Guaranteed convergence**: BGD is guaranteed to converge to theglobal minimum of the loss function if the learning rate is sufficiently small. * **Simple to implement**: BGD is easy to understand and implement.

However, BGD has some disadvantages:
*   **Computationally expensive**: Computing the gradient using the entiredataset can be computationally expensive, especially for large datasets. * **Slow convergence**: BGD can converge slowly, especially if the dataset is large and the learning rate is small.

Stochastic Gradient Descent (SGD)
Stochastic Gradient Descent is a variant of Gradient Descent that considers one example from the dataset at a time to compute the gradient of the loss function. Here's a step-by-step overview of SGD:

1.   **Select a random example**: Select a random example from thedataset.

2.   **Compute the gradient**: Calculate the gradient of the loss function withrespect to the model's parameters using the selected example.

3.   **Update the parameters**: Update the model's parameters bysubtracting the product of the learning rate and the computed gradient.

4.   **Repeat**: Repeat steps 1-3 until convergence or a stopping criterion isreached.

The advantages of SGD are:

*   **Fast computation**: Computing the gradient using one example is muchfaster than computing the gradient using the entire dataset.

*   **Faster convergence**: SGD can converge faster than BGD, especiallyfor large datasets.

However, SGD has some disadvantages:

*   **Noisy updates**: The updates in SGD can be noisy, which can lead toslower convergence or oscillations.

*   **Not guaranteed to converge**: SGD is not guaranteed to converge tothe global minimum of the loss function, especially if the learning rate is not properly tuned.

Mini-Batch Gradient Descent (MBGD)

Mini-Batch Gradient Descent is a variant of Gradient Descent that considers a small batch of examples from the dataset at a time to compute the gradient of the loss function. Here's a step-by-step overview of MBGD:

1.   **Select a mini-batch**: Select a small batch of examples from thedataset.

2.   **Compute the gradient**: Calculate the gradient of the loss function withrespect to the model's parameters using the selected mini-batch.

3.   **Update the parameters**: Update the model's parameters bysubtracting the product of the learning rate and the computed gradient.

4.   **Repeat**: Repeat steps 1-3 until convergence or a stopping criterion isreached.

The advantages of MBGD are:

*   **Balances computation and noise**: MBGD balances the computationrequired to compute the gradient and the noise in the updates.

*   **Faster convergence**: MBGD can converge faster than BGD and SGD,especially for large datasets.

However, MBGD has some disadvantages:

*   **Requires tuning**: The size of the mini-batch requires tuning, which canbe time-consuming.
*   **Not guaranteed to converge**: MBGD is not guaranteed to converge tothe global minimum of the loss function, especially if the learning rate is not properly tuned.

In summary, the choice of Gradient Descent variant depends on the size of the dataset, the computational resources available, and the desired trade-off between computation and convergence speed.

Q: Explain multivariate distribution in data science.

A: **Multivariate Distribution in Data Science**

===

In data science, a multivariate distribution is a probability distribution that describes the joint behavior of multiple random variables. It is a fundamental concept in statistics and machine learning, as it allows us to model and analyze complex relationships between multiple variables.

Definition

A multivariate distribution is a probability distribution that assigns a probability to each possible combination of values for a set of random variables. It is characterized by a joint probability density function (PDF) or joint probability mass function (PMF), which describes the probability of observing a particular combination of values for the variables.

Key Concepts

----

1.   **Marginal Distribution**: The marginal distribution of a single variable isthe probability distribution of that variable, ignoring the values of the other variables.
2.   **Conditional Distribution**: The conditional distribution of a variablegiven the values of other variables is the probability distribution of that variable, given that the other variables have taken on specific values.
3.   **Joint Distribution**: The joint distribution of multiple variables is theprobability distribution that describes the joint behavior of all the variables. 4. **Covariance**: The covariance between two variables measures the linear relationship between them.
5. **Correlation**: The correlation between two variables measures the strength and direction of the linear relationship between them.

Types of Multivariate Distributions

----

1.   **Multivariate Normal Distribution**: A distribution where each variablefollows a normal distribution, and the joint distribution is also normal.
2.   **Multivariate Student's t-Distribution**: A distribution where eachvariable follows a Student's t-distribution, and the joint distribution is also a Student's t-distribution.
3.   **Multivariate Exponential Distribution**: A distribution where eachvariable follows an exponential distribution, and the joint distribution is also an exponential distribution.
4.   **Multivariate Dirichlet Distribution**: A distribution where each variablefollows a Dirichlet distribution, and the joint distribution is also a Dirichlet distribution.

Applications

----

1.   **Regression Analysis**: Multivariate distributions are used to model therelationships between multiple predictor variables and a response variable.
2.   **Cluster Analysis**: Multivariate distributions are used to identify clustersor groups of similar observations in a dataset.
3.   **Dimensionality Reduction**: Multivariate distributions are used toreduce the dimensionality of a dataset, while preserving the most important information.
4.   **Anomaly Detection**: Multivariate distributions are used to detectanomalies or outliers in a dataset.

Example Use Case

Suppose we have a dataset of exam scores for students, with variables for math, science, and English scores. We can use a multivariate normal distribution to model the joint behavior of these variables, and then use this model to:

* Predict the probability of a student scoring above a certain threshold on allthree exams
* Identify clusters of students with similar score profiles
* Reduce the dimensionality of the dataset, while preserving the mostimportant information

Code Example

Here is an example of how to use a multivariate normal distribution in Python using the `scipy` library:
```python
import
numpy as np
from scipy.stats import multivariate_normal
# Define the mean and covariance matrix of the multivariate normal distribution
mean = np.array([0, 0, 0])
cov = np.array([[1, 0.5, 0.2], [0.5, 1, 0.3], [0.2, 0.3, 1]])

# Create a multivariate normal distribution object mvn =
multivariate_normal(mean, cov)

# Generate a random sample from the distribution sample =
mvn.rvs(100)

# Print the sample
print(sample)
```

This code defines a multivariate normal distribution with a mean vector and covariance matrix, and then generates a random sample from the distribution.

Q: What is a loss function, and how do you choose the appropriate one for your model?

A: A loss function, also known as a cost function or objective function, is a mathematical function that measures the difference between the model's predictions and the actual true values. It is used to evaluate the performance of a model during the training process, and its primary goal is to minimize the difference between predictions and true values.

Why is a loss function necessary?

A loss function is necessary for several reasons:

1.   **Model evaluation**: A loss function provides a way to evaluate theperformance of a model during training, allowing you to monitor its progress and adjust the model as needed.
2.   **Optimization**: A loss function is used as the objective function inoptimization algorithms, such as gradient descent, to minimize the difference between predictions and true values.

3.   **Hyperparameter   tuning**:   A   loss   function
    helps   to   tune hyperparameters, such as learning rates, regularization
strengths, and batch sizes, to improve the model's performance.

Common loss functions
Some common loss functions used in machine learning are:

1.   **Mean Squared Error (MSE)**: measures the average squareddifference
between predictions and true values.
2.   **Mean Absolute Error (MAE)**: measures the average absolutedifference
between predictions and true values.
3.   **Cross-Entropy   Loss**:   measures   the   difference   between
predictedprobabilities and true labels, commonly used in classification problems.
4.   **Binary Cross-Entropy Loss**: measures the difference betweenpredicted
probabilities and true labels in binary classification problems.
5.   **Kullback-Leibler   Divergence**:   measures   the   difference   between
twoprobability distributions.

Choosing the appropriate loss function

To choose the appropriate loss function for your model, consider the following
factors:

1.   **Problem type**: Different loss functions are suited for different
problemtypes, such as regression, classification, or clustering.
2.   **Data distribution**: The loss function should be chosen based on
thedistribution of the data, such as Gaussian, Poisson, or categorical.
3.   **Model architecture**: The loss function should be compatible with
themodel architecture, such as linear, logistic, or neural networks.
4.   **Evaluation metric**: The loss function should be aligned with
theevaluation metric used to measure the model's performance, such as accuracy,
precision, or recall.
5.   **Robustness to outliers**: The loss function should be robust to outliersand
anomalies in the data.

Example

Suppose you are building a regression model to predict house prices. In this case, you
might choose the Mean Squared Error (MSE) loss function, as it is commonly used for
regression problems and is sensitive to the magnitude of the errors.

However, if you are building a classification model to predict whether a customer will buy a product or not, you might choose the Binary Cross-Entropy Loss function, as it is well-suited for binary classification problems and is sensitive to the probability of the positive class.

In summary, choosing the appropriate loss function is crucial for training a model that generalizes well to new, unseen data. By considering the problem type, data distribution, model architecture, evaluation metric, and robustness to outliers, you can select a loss function that aligns with your model's goals and objectives.

Q: What is difference between object detections and image segmentations.

A: Object detection and image segmentation are two fundamental tasks in the field of computer vision. While they are related, they serve different purposes and have distinct differences:

Object Detection:

Object detection involves locating and classifying objects within an image or video. The goal is to identify the presence, location, and category of objects, such as people, cars, animals, or objects. Object detection typically outputs:

1. Bounding boxes: Rectangular regions surrounding the detected objects.
2. Class labels: The category or class of the detected object (e.g., person,car, dog).
3. Confidence scores: The probability of the detection being correct.

Object detection is commonly used in applications such as:

* Surveillance systems
* Autonomous vehicles
* Image search
* Facial recognition

Image Segmentation:

Image segmentation involves dividing an image into its constituent parts or objects, where each pixel is assigned a label or class. The goal is to identify the precise boundaries and shapes of objects within the image. Image segmentation typically outputs:

1. Pixel-wise masks: A binary mask or a set of binary masks, where eachmask corresponds to a specific object or class.

2. Class labels: The category or class of each pixel or region.

Image segmentation is commonly used in applications such as:
* Medical imaging (e.g., tumor detection, organ segmentation)
* Autonomous vehicles (e.g., lane detection, road segmentation)
* Robotics (e.g., object manipulation, scene understanding)
* Satellite imaging (e.g., land cover classification, change detection)

Key differences:

1.   **Granularity**: Object detection provides a coarse representation ofobjects, whereas image segmentation provides a fine-grained, pixel-level representation.
2.   **Output**: Object detection outputs bounding boxes and class labels,while image segmentation outputs pixel-wise masks and class labels.
3.   **Purpose**: Object detection is often used for tasks that requiredetecting and recognizing objects, while image segmentation is used for tasks that require understanding the precise boundaries and shapes of objects.
4.   **Complexity**: Image segmentation is generally more complex andcomputationally intensive than object detection, as it requires assigning a label to each pixel in the image.

In summary, object detection is a more general task that focuses on detecting and recognizing objects, while image segmentation is a more specific task that focuses on understanding the precise boundaries and shapes of objects. Both tasks are essential in computer vision, and the choice of task depends on the specific application and requirements.

Q: Explain the concept of word embeddings in natural language processing (NLP).

A: **Introduction to Word Embeddings**
=====================================

Word embeddings are a fundamental concept in natural language processing (NLP) that represents words as vectors in a high-dimensional space. This allows words with similar meanings to be mapped to nearby points in the vector space, enabling computers to understand the semantic relationships between words.

What are Word Embeddings?

Word embeddings are a type of word representation that uses a dense vector to represent each word in a vocabulary. These vectors are learned from large amounts of text data and capture the context in which words are used. The goal of word embeddings is to map words to a vector space such that:

* Words with similar meanings are close together
* Words with different meanings are far apart
* Words with related meanings are clustered together

How are Word Embeddings Learned?

Word embeddings are typically learned using neural network-based models, such as:

1.   **Word2Vec**: A popular algorithm for learning word embeddings, introduced by Mikolov et al. in 2013. Word2Vec uses a neural network to predict the context words surrounding a given word.
2.   **GloVe**: Another popular algorithm for learning word embeddings, introduced by Pennington et al. in 2014. GloVe uses a matrix factorization technique to learn word embeddings.

These models learn word embeddings by optimizing an objective function that measures the similarity between words and their contexts. The resulting word embeddings can be used as input features for various NLP tasks, such as text classification, sentiment analysis, and language modeling.

Properties of Word Embeddings

Word embeddings have several interesting properties:

*   **Semantic similarity**: Words with similar meanings are close together inthe vector space.
*   **Analogies**: Word embeddings can capture analogies between words,such as "king" is to "man" as "queen" is to "woman".
*   **Compositionality**: Word embeddings can be combined to representphrases or sentences.

Applications of Word Embeddings

Word embeddings have a wide range of applications in NLP, including:

* **Text classification**: Word embeddings can be used as input featuresfor text classification tasks, such as spam detection or sentiment analysis. * **Language modeling**: Word embeddings can be used to improve language modeling tasks, such as predicting the next word in a sentence. * **Information retrieval**: Word embeddings can be used to improve search engines by capturing the semantic meaning of search queries.

Conclusion

Word embeddings are a powerful tool for representing words in a vector space, enabling computers to understand the semantic relationships between words. By learning word embeddings from large amounts of text data, we can improve the performance of various NLP tasks and applications.

Q: What is tokenization? Give me a difference between lemmatization and stemming?

A: **Tokenization:**
Tokenization is the process of breaking down text into individual words or tokens. It's a fundamental step in natural language processing (NLP) and is used to split text into smaller units, such as words, phrases, or characters, that can be analyzed and processed separately. Tokenization can be performed using various techniques, including:

* Word-level tokenization (splitting text into individual words)
* Sentence-level tokenization (splitting text into individual sentences)* Subword-level tokenization (splitting words into subwords, such as word pieces or character sequences)

Lemmatization vs. Stemming:
Both lemmatization and stemming are techniques used to reduce words to their base or root form, but they differ in their approach and outcome:

* **Stemming:** Stemming involves removing the suffixes from words toobtain a reduced form, which is called the stem. For example, the words "running", "runs", and "runner" would all be reduced to the stem "run". However, stemming can be simplistic and may not always produce the correct base form of a word. For instance, the word "happiness" would be reduced to "happi", which is not a valid word.

* **Lemmatization:** Lemmatization, on the other hand, uses adictionary-based approach to reduce words to their base or root form, known as the lemma. Lemmatization takes into account the context and meaning of the word, as well as its grammatical category (such as noun, verb, adjective, etc.). For example, the words "running", "runs", and "runner" would all be reduced to the lemma "run", while the word "happiness" would be reduced to the lemma "happy".

The key differences between lemmatization and stemming are:

* **Accuracy:** Lemmatization is generally more accurate than stemming,as it uses a dictionary-based approach to determine the base form of a word.
* **Contextual understanding:** Lemmatization takes into account thecontext and meaning of the word, while stemming relies solely on the suffixes.
* **Output:** Lemmatization produces a valid word (the lemma), whilestemming may produce an invalid or incomplete word (the stem).

In summary, tokenization is the process of breaking down text into individual words or tokens, while lemmatization and stemming are techniques used to reduce words to their base or root form. Lemmatization is a more accurate and context-aware approach than stemming, producing a valid word (the lemma) as output.

Q: Explain the concept of Bag of Words (BoW) and its limitations.

A: **Bag of Words (BoW) Concept:**
The Bag of Words (BoW) is a simple and widely used text representation technique in Natural Language Processing (NLP). It represents a document or text as a bag, or a set, of its word occurrences without considering the order or grammar of the words. Each document is represented as a vector, where each element in the vector corresponds to the frequency of a particular word in the document.

How BoW Works:

1. **Tokenization**: The text is broken down into individual words or tokens.
2. **Stopword removal**: Common words like "the", "and", etc. are removedas they do not carry much meaning.
3. **Stemming or Lemmatization**: Words are reduced to their base form toreduce dimensionality.
4. **Vector representation**: A vector is created for each document, whereeach element represents the frequency of a word in the document.

Example:

Suppose we have two documents:

Doc1: "The cat sat on the mat"
Doc2: "The dog ran on the mat"

The BoW representation for these documents would be:

Word	Doc1	Doc2
the	2	2
cat	1	0
sat	1	0
on	1	1
mat	1	1
dog	0	1
ran	0	1

Limitations of BoW:

1.   **Loss of word order**: BoW does not consider the order of words, whichcan lead to loss of semantic meaning.
2.   **No context**: BoW does not capture the context in which a word isused, which can lead to ambiguity.
3.   **High dimensionality**: The vector representation can be veryhigh-dimensional, leading to computational complexity and overfitting.
4.   **No handling of out-of-vocabulary words**: BoW does not handle wordsthat are not in the training vocabulary.
5.   **No capture of nuances**: BoW does not capture nuances likesynonyms, antonyms, or hyponyms.
6.   **Sensitive to noise**: BoW is sensitive to noise in the data, such astypos or irrelevant words.

Alternatives and Improvements:
To address these limitations, several alternatives and improvements have been proposed, including:

1.   **Term Frequency-Inverse Document Frequency (TF-IDF)**: weightsword frequencies by importance in the entire corpus.
2.   **Word embeddings**: represents words as dense vectors in alower-dimensional space, capturing semantic relationships.

3.   **N-grams**: considers sequences of words, capturing some context andword order information.

4.   **Deep learning models**: uses neural networks to learn complexrepresentations of text, capturing nuances and context.

In summary, while BoW is a simple and effective technique for text representation, its limitations can be addressed by using more advanced techniques that capture context, semantics, and nuances of language.

Q: What is word embedding, and why is it useful in NLP?

A: **Word Embedding: A Fundamental Concept in NLP**
==

Word embedding is a technique used in Natural Language Processing (NLP) to represent words or phrases as vectors in a high-dimensional space. This allows words with similar meanings to be mapped to nearby points in the vector space, enabling machines to capture semantic relationships between words.

What is Word Embedding?

Word embedding is a way to represent words as numerical vectors, called word vectors or word embeddings, in a way that preserves their semantic meaning. Each word is assigned a unique vector in a high-dimensional space, typically with hundreds or thousands of dimensions. The vectors are learned from large amounts of text data, such as books, articles, or websites, using various algorithms.

How is Word Embedding Useful in NLP?

Word embedding is useful in NLP for several reasons:

1.   **Captures semantic relationships**: Word embeddings can capturenuanced relationships between words, such as synonyms, antonyms, hyponyms, and analogies.

2.   **Improves text classification**: Word embeddings can be used as inputfeatures for text classification models, such as sentiment analysis, spam detection, and topic modeling.

3.   **Enhances language modeling**: Word embeddings can be used topredict the next word in a sentence, given the context of the previous words.

4.   **Facilitates machine translation**: Word embeddings can be used totranslate text from one language to another, by learning to map words from one language to their equivalents in another language.

5.   **Supports information retrieval**: Word embeddings can be used toimprove search engines, by allowing them to understand the semantic meaning of search queries and retrieve relevant documents.

Popular Word Embedding Algorithms

Some popular word embedding algorithms include:

1.   **Word2Vec**: A widely used algorithm that uses neural networks tolearn word embeddings.

2.   **GloVe**: An algorithm that uses matrix factorization to learn wordembeddings.

3.   **FastText**: An algorithm that uses subword modeling to learn wordembeddings.

Example Use Cases

----

1.   **Sentiment analysis**: Use word embeddings to analyze the sentimentof text data, such as movie reviews or customer feedback.

2.   **Text summarization**: Use word embeddings to summarize longdocuments, such as news articles or books.

3.   **Language translation**: Use word embeddings to translate text fromone language to another, such as English to Spanish.

In summary, word embedding is a powerful technique in NLP that allows machines to capture the semantic meaning of words and phrases, enabling a wide range of applications in text analysis, language modeling, and machine translation.

Q: How does TF-IDF work, and how is it different from simple word frequency?

A: **TF-IDF Overview** ===============

TF-IDF (Term Frequency-Inverse Document Frequency) is a widely used technique in natural language processing (NLP) and information retrieval for calculating the importance of words in a document. It takes into account two factors:

1. **Term Frequency (TF)**: The frequency of a word in a document.

2. **Inverse Document Frequency (IDF)**: The rarity of a word across a collection of documents.

Term Frequency (TF)

TF is a measure of how often a word appears in a document. It is calculated as the number of times a word appears in a document divided by the total number of words in the document.

Inverse Document Frequency (IDF)

IDF is a measure of how rare a word is across a collection of documents. It is calculated as the logarithm of the total number of documents divided by the number of documents containing the word.

TF-IDF Calculation

The TF-IDF score is calculated by multiplying the TF and IDF scores.

TF-IDF = TF * IDF

Example

Suppose we have a collection of documents, and we want to calculate the TF-IDF score for the word "machine" in a document.

Document	Words	"machine" Frequency
Doc1	100	5
Doc2	150	2
Doc3	200	0

TF = 5/100 = 0.05 (in Doc1)
IDF = log(3/2) = 0.176 (across the collection)
TF-IDF = 0.05 * 0.176 = 0.0088

Difference from Simple Word Frequency

Simple word frequency only considers the frequency of a word in a document, without taking into account its rarity across a collection of documents. TF-IDF, on the other hand, considers both the frequency of a word in a document and its rarity across a collection of documents.

This makes TF-IDF a more effective technique for:

*   **Weighting word importance**: TF-IDF gives more weight to rare wordsthat are more likely to be important for the document's meaning.
*   **Reducing noise**: TF-IDF reduces the impact of common words (like"the", "and", etc.) that do not add much value to the document's meaning.

Code Example (Python)

```python
import numpy as np from
collections import Counter import
math

def calculate_tf(word, document):
    """
    Calculate the term frequency of a word in a document.

    Args:
        word (str): The word to calculate the TF for.       document
(list): The list of words in the document.

    Returns:
        float: The term frequency of the word.
    """
    word_count = Counter(document)
    tf = word_count[word] / len(document)    return tf

def calculate_idf(word, documents):
    """
    Calculate the inverse document frequency of a word across a collection of
documents.

    Args:
```

```
    word (str): The word to calculate the IDF for.        documents
(list): The list of documents.

    Returns:
        float: The inverse document frequency of the word.
    """
    num_docs = len(documents)
    num_docs_with_word = sum(1 for doc in documents if word in doc)        idf =
math.log(num_docs / num_docs_with_word)
    return idf

def calculate_tf_idf(word, document, documents):
    """
    Calculate the TF-IDF score of a word in a document.

    Args:
        word (str): The word to calculate the TF-IDF for.        document
(list): The list of words in the document.        documents (list): The list
of documents.

    Returns:
        float: The TF-IDF score of the word.
    """
    tf = calculate_tf(word, document)
    idf = calculate_idf(word, documents)
    tf_idf = tf * idf        return
tf_idf

# Example usage
document = ["machine", "learning", "is", "a", "field", "of", "study"] documents = [
    ["machine", "learning", "is", "a", "field", "of", "study"],
    ["machine", "learning", "is", "used", "in", "many", "applications"],
    ["natural", "language", "processing", "is", "a", "field", "of", "study"]
]

word = "machine"
tf_idf = calculate_tf_idf(word, document, documents)
print(f"TF-IDF score for '{word}': {tf_idf}") ```
```

In this example, we define three functions to calculate the TF, IDF, and TF-IDF scores. We then use these functions to calculate the TF-IDF score for the word "machine" in a document.

Q: What is Named Entity Recognition (NER), and where is it applied?

A: Named Entity Recognition (NER) is a subtask of Natural Language Processing (NLP) that involves identifying and categorizing named entities in unstructured text into predefined categories. These categories may include:

1. **Person**: names of individuals, such as "John Smith" or "AlbertEinstein".
2. **Organization**: names of companies, institutions, or teams, such as"Google" or "Harvard University".
3. **Location**: names of places, such as "New York City" or "London".
4. **Date**: dates, such as "January 1, 2022" or "2020".
5. **Time**: times, such as "10:00 AM" or "2:00 PM".
6. **Event**: names of events, such as "World Cup" or "Olympics".
7. **Product**: names of products, such as "iPhone" or "Toyota Camry".

The goal of NER is to extract these entities from text and classify them into their respective categories, allowing for easier analysis, searching, and understanding of the text.

NER has numerous applications in various fields, including:

1.   **Information Retrieval**: NER helps improve search engine results byidentifying and categorizing relevant entities in search queries.
2.   **Text Summarization**: NER assists in summarizing long documents byextracting key entities and their relationships.
3.   **Sentiment Analysis**: NER helps analyze sentiment by identifyingentities and their associated opinions or emotions.
4.   **Question Answering**: NER enables question answering systems toidentify and extract relevant entities from text.
5.   **Data Mining**: NER facilitates data mining by extracting andcategorizing entities from large datasets.
6.   **Speech Recognition**: NER is used in speech recognition systems toimprove the accuracy of entity recognition in spoken language.
7.   **Machine Translation**: NER helps machine translation systems tobetter understand and translate text by identifying and categorizing entities.

8. **Social Media Monitoring**: NER is used to analyze and extract insightsfrom social media data, such as identifying trending topics or sentiment towards specific entities.

Some real-world examples of NER applications include:

*   Google's search engine, which uses NER to identify and categorizeentities in search queries.
*   Facebook's entity recognition, which identifies and categorizes entities inuser posts and comments.
*   Amazon's product search, which uses NER to identify and categorizeproduct names and descriptions.

In summary, Named Entity Recognition is a fundamental NLP task that has numerous applications in various fields, enabling the extraction and categorization of entities from unstructured text, and improving the accuracy and efficiency of various NLP tasks.

Q: How does Latent Dirichlet Allocation (LDA) work for topic modeling?

A: Latent Dirichlet Allocation (LDA) is a popular topic modeling technique used to discover hidden topics in a large corpus of text data. It's a generative model that represents documents as mixtures of topics, where each topic is a distribution over a fixed vocabulary of words.

Key Concepts:

1. **Documents**: A collection of text documents, each represented as abag-of-words (a set of words without considering their order or grammar).
2. **Topics**: A set of latent topics, each represented as a distribution overthe vocabulary of words.
3. **Words**: The individual words in the vocabulary.

LDA Model:

The LDA model consists of the following components:

1.   **Document-Topic Distribution**: Each document is represented as amixture of topics, where the mixture is defined by a probability distribution over the topics (?).
2.   **Topic-Word Distribution**: Each topic is represented as a probabilitydistribution over the vocabulary of words (?).

3.   **Word-Topic Assignment**: Each word in a document is assigned to atopic, based on the document-topic distribution and the topic-word distribution.

Inference Process:

The LDA model is typically inferred using a Bayesian approach, which involves the following steps:

1.   **Initialize**: Initialize the document-topic distribution (?) and topic-worddistribution (?) with random values.
2.   **E-Step**: For each document, compute the posterior distribution overtopics for each word, based on the current estimates of ? and ?.
3.   **M-Step**: Update the document-topic distribution (?) and topic-worddistribution (?) based on the posterior distributions computed in the E-Step. 4. **Repeat**: Repeat the E-Step and M-Step until convergence or a stopping criterion is reached.

Output:

The output of the LDA model is a set of topics, each represented as a distribution over the vocabulary of words. The topics are often visualized using word clouds or topic-word matrices, which show the most important words in each topic.

Example:

Suppose we have a corpus of text documents about sports, politics, and entertainment. The LDA model might discover the following topics:

* Topic 1: Sports (words: football, basketball, stadium, player)
* Topic 2: Politics (words: government, election, policy, president)* Topic 3: Entertainment (words: movie, music, actor, actress)

Each document in the corpus would be represented as a mixture of these topics, with a probability distribution over the topics. For example, a document about a sports movie might have a high probability of belonging to both the Sports and Entertainment topics.

Advantages:

1. **Unsupervised**: LDA is an unsupervised technique, meaning it doesn'trequire labeled data.

2. **Flexible**: LDA can handle large and complex datasets.
3. **Interpretable**: The topics discovered by LDA are often interpretableand meaningful.

Limitations:

1.   **Computational Complexity**: LDA can be computationally expensive,especially for large datasets.
2.   **Hyperparameter Tuning**: LDA requires tuning of hyperparameters,such as the number of topics and the prior distributions.
3.   **Overfitting**: LDA can suffer from overfitting, especially when thenumber of topics is too large.

Q: How do you handle out-of-vocabulary (OOV) words in NLP models?

A: Handling out-of-vocabulary (OOV) words is a common challenge in Natural Language Processing (NLP) models. OOV words are words that are not present in the training data or vocabulary of the model. Here are some strategies to handle OOV words:

1.   **Subwording**: This involves breaking down words into subwords orword pieces. For example, the word "unbreakable" can be broken down into "un", "break", and "able". This helps to reduce the number of OOV words and improves the model's ability to handle rare or unseen words.
2.   **Character-level modeling**: This involves modeling words at thecharacter level, rather than the word level. This can help to handle OOV words by representing them as a sequence of characters.
3.   **Word embeddings**: Word embeddings, such as Word2Vec or GloVe,can be used to represent words as vectors in a high-dimensional space. These vectors can be used to represent OOV words by using the vector representation of the closest in-vocabulary word.
4.   **Unknown word token**: Many NLP models use a special token, such as`<UNK>`, to represent OOV words. This token can be used as a placeholder for any OOV word, and the model can learn to represent it as a vector.
5.   **Vocabulary expansion**: This involves expanding the vocabulary of themodel by adding new words to the training data. This can be done by using external resources, such as dictionaries or thesauri, to add new words to the vocabulary.
6.   **Transfer learning**: Transfer learning involves using a pre-trainedmodel as a starting point for a new task. This can help to handle OOV words by leveraging the knowledge learned by the pre-trained model.

7.   **Named Entity Recognition (NER)**: NER can be used to identify andextract named entities, such as names, locations, and organizations, which are often OOV words.

8.   **Part-of-speech (POS) tagging**: POS tagging can be used to identifythe part of speech of a word, which can help to disambiguate OOV words.

9.   **Language modeling**: Language modeling can be used to predict theprobability of a word given the context. This can help to handle OOV words by predicting the probability of the word given the context.

10.   **Ensemble methods**: Ensemble methods, such as bagging orboosting, can be used to combine the predictions of multiple models. This can help to improve the handling of OOV words by leveraging the strengths of multiple models.

Some popular techniques for handling OOV words include:

*   **FastText**: FastText is a library for text classification and languagemodeling that uses subwording and word embeddings to handle OOV words.

*   **BERT**: BERT is a pre-trained language model that uses subwordingand word embeddings to handle OOV words.

*   **WordPiece**: WordPiece is a tokenization algorithm that breaks downwords into subwords, which can help to handle OOV words.

Overall, the choice of technique for handling OOV words depends on the specific task, dataset, and model architecture.

Q: Explain the concept of attention mechanisms and their role in sequence-to-sequence tasks.

A: Attention mechanisms are a key component in sequence-to-sequence tasks, which involve mapping a sequence of inputs (e.g., words, characters, or tokens) to a sequence of outputs (e.g., translated text, generated text, or predicted labels). The primary goal of attention mechanisms is to enable the model to focus on specific parts of the input sequence when generating each output element.

What is an Attention Mechanism?

An attention mechanism is a neural network component that allows the model to weigh the importance of different input elements when computing the output. It's a way to selectively concentrate on specific parts of the input sequence, rather than treating all elements equally. This is particularly useful when dealing with long input sequences, where not all elements are equally relevant to the output.

How Does Attention Work?

The attention mechanism works as follows:

1.   **Compute attention weights**: The model computes a set of attentionweights, which represent the importance of each input element. These weights are typically computed based on the input elements and the current output element being generated.
2.   **Compute context vector**: The attention weights are used to compute acontext vector, which is a weighted sum of the input elements. The context vector represents the most relevant information from the input sequence for the current output element.
3.   **Use context vector**: The context vector is used to compute the outputelement, often in conjunction with other model components, such as recurrent neural networks (RNNs) or transformers.

Types of Attention Mechanisms

There are several types of attention mechanisms, including:

1.   **Global attention**: This type of attention computes attention weights forall input elements and uses them to compute the context vector.
2.   **Local attention**: This type of attention computes attention weights fora fixed-size window of input elements and uses them to compute the context vector.
3.   **Hierarchical attention**: This type of attention computes attentionweights at multiple levels of granularity, such as words, phrases, and sentences.

Role in Sequence-to-Sequence Tasks

Attention mechanisms play a crucial role in sequence-to-sequence tasks, such as:

1.   **Machine translation**: Attention mechanisms help the model focus onthe most relevant words in the source language when generating the translated text.
2.   **Text summarization**: Attention mechanisms help the model identifythe most important sentences or phrases in the input text when generating a summary.
3.   **Chatbots**: Attention mechanisms help the model focus on the mostrelevant parts of the user's input when generating a response.

Benefits of Attention Mechanisms

Attention mechanisms offer several benefits, including:

1.   **Improved performance**: Attention mechanisms can improve theperformance of sequence-to-sequence models by allowing them to focus on the most relevant input elements.
2.   **Increased interpretability**: Attention mechanisms can provide insightsinto which input elements are most important for the model's predictions.
3.   **Reduced computational complexity**: Attention mechanisms canreduce the computational complexity of sequence-to-sequence models by allowing them to focus on a subset of the input elements.

In summary, attention mechanisms are a powerful tool for sequence-to-sequence tasks, enabling models to selectively focus on specific parts of the input sequence when generating output elements. By computing attention weights and using them to compute context vectors, attention mechanisms can improve the performance, interpretability, and efficiency of sequence-to-sequence models.

Q: How does BERT work, and what makes it different from previous NLP models?

A: BERT (Bidirectional Encoder Representations from Transformers) is a pre-trained language model developed by Google in 2018. It revolutionized the field of Natural Language Processing (NLP) by achieving state-of-the-art results in various NLP tasks. Here's how BERT works and what makes it different from previous NLP models:

Architecture:

BERT is built on top of the Transformer architecture, which is a type of neural network designed primarily for sequence-to-sequence tasks. The Transformer consists of an encoder and a decoder. BERT uses only the encoder part of the Transformer, which is responsible for generating contextualized representations of input words.

Training:

BERT is pre-trained on a large corpus of text, such as the entire Wikipedia and BookCorpus. The pre-training process involves two tasks:

1.   **Masked Language Modeling (MLM):** Some of the input words arerandomly replaced with a [MASK] token, and the model is trained to predict the original word.
2.   **Next Sentence Prediction (NSP):** The model is trained to predictwhether two sentences are adjacent in the original text.

These two tasks help BERT learn to capture contextual relationships between words and sentences.

Key Features:

1.   **Bidirectional Training:** Unlike previous models, which were trainedusing left-to-right or right-to-left approaches, BERT is trained using a bidirectional approach. This means that the model considers both the left and right context of a word when generating its representation.
2.   **Contextualized Embeddings:** BERT generates contextualizedembeddings for each word in the input sequence. These embeddings capture the nuances of word meaning based on the context in which they appear.
3.   **Pre-training:** BERT is pre-trained on a large corpus of text, whichallows it to learn general language patterns and relationships. This pre-training step is crucial for achieving state-of-the-art results in various NLP tasks.

What makes BERT different:

1.   **Improved Contextual Understanding:** BERT's bidirectional trainingand contextualized embeddings enable it to capture complex contextual relationships between words, which was not possible with previous models.
2.   **Pre-training:** BERT's pre-training step allows it to learn generallanguage patterns and relationships, making it a more versatile and effective model for various NLP tasks.
3.   **Fine-tuning:** BERT can be fine-tuned for specific NLP tasks, such asquestion answering, sentiment analysis, and text classification, by adding a task-specific layer on top of the pre-trained model.

Impact:

BERT has achieved state-of-the-art results in various NLP tasks, including:

1.   **Question Answering:** BERT has achieved state-of-the-art results inquestion answering tasks, such as SQuAD and TriviaQA.
2.   **Sentiment Analysis:** BERT has achieved state-of-the-art results insentiment analysis tasks, such as IMDB and SST-2.
3.   **Text Classification:** BERT has achieved state-of-the-art results in textclassification tasks, such as 20 Newsgroups and AG News.

Overall, BERT's innovative architecture, pre-training approach, and fine-tuning capabilities have made it a powerful and versatile model for various NLP tasks.

Q: How is the transformer different from RNN and LSTM?

A: The Transformer, RNN (Recurrent Neural Network), and LSTM (Long Short-Term Memory) are all types of neural network architectures used for sequence-to-sequence tasks, such as language translation, text generation, and speech recognition. While they share some similarities, they differ significantly in their design and functionality.

RNN (Recurrent Neural Network)

RNNs are a type of neural network designed to handle sequential data, where each input is dependent on the previous ones. They maintain a hidden state that captures information from previous inputs, allowing them to keep track of context and make predictions based on that context. However, RNNs have some limitations:

1.   **Vanishing gradients**: As the sequence length increases, the gradientsused to update the weights during backpropagation become smaller, making it difficult to train the network.
2.   **Sequential computation**: RNNs process inputs one at a time, whichcan be slow for long sequences.

LSTM (Long Short-Term Memory)

LSTMs are a type of RNN designed to address the limitations of traditional RNNs. They introduce a memory cell and three gates (input, output, and forget gates) to control the flow of information:

1.   **Memory cell**: Stores information for long periods, allowing the networkto capture long-term dependencies.
2.   **Gates**: Regulate the flow of information into and out of the memorycell, helping to prevent vanishing gradients.

LSTMs are more effective than traditional RNNs, but they still have some limitations:

1.   **Sequential computation**: Like RNNs, LSTMs process inputs one at atime, which can be slow for long sequences.
2.   **Limited parallelization**: Due to their sequential nature, LSTMs aredifficult to parallelize, making them less efficient for large-scale computations.

Transformer

The Transformer, introduced in 2017, revolutionized the field of natural language processing (NLP) by replacing traditional RNNs and LSTMs with a novel architecture:

1.   **Self-attention mechanism**: The Transformer uses self-attention toweigh the importance of different input elements relative to each other, allowing it to capture long-range dependencies more efficiently.
2.   **Parallelization**: The Transformer can be parallelized more easily thanRNNs and LSTMs, making it much faster for large-scale computations.
3.   **Encoder-decoder structure**: The Transformer consists of an encoderand a decoder, each composed of a stack of identical layers. The encoder takes in a sequence of tokens (e.g., words or characters) and outputs a sequence of vectors, which are then used by the decoder to generate the output sequence.

Key differences between the Transformer and RNN/LSTM:

1.   **Parallelization**: The Transformer can be parallelized more easily,making it faster for large-scale computations.
2.   **Self-attention**: The Transformer uses self-attention to capturelong-range dependencies, while RNNs and LSTMs rely on recurrent connections and gates.
3.   **Non-sequential computation**: The Transformer processes all inputelements simultaneously, whereas RNNs and LSTMs process them one at a time.

In summary, the Transformer is a more efficient and effective architecture for sequence-to-sequence tasks, especially for long-range dependencies and large-scale computations. While RNNs and LSTMs are still useful for certain applications, the Transformer has become the go-to architecture for many NLP tasks.

Q: How does self-attention work?

A: Self-attention is a key component of the Transformer architecture, introduced in the paper "Attention is All You Need" by Vaswani et al. in 2017. It's a mechanism that allows the model to attend to different parts of the input sequence simultaneously and weigh their importance.

Basic Idea:

Self-attention is a way to compute a weighted sum of the input elements, where the weights are learned based on the input elements themselves. The goal is to capture the relationships between different parts of the input sequence, such as words in a sentence.

Mathematical Formulation:

Given an input sequence of vectors `x = (x1, x2, ..., xn)`, self-attention computes the output `z` as follows:

1. **Query, Key, and Value**: First, the input sequence is linearly transformed into three vectors: `Q` (query), `K` (key), and `V` (value). These vectors are obtained by applying different learnable linear transformations to the input sequence:
* `Q = x * W_Q`
* `K = x * W_K`
* `V = x * W_V`
2. **Attention Scores**: Compute the attention scores by taking the dot product of `Q` and `K` and applying a scaling factor:
* `A = Q * K^T / sqrt(d)`
* `d` is the dimensionality of the input vectors
3. **Softmax**: Apply a softmax function to the attention scores to obtain a probability distribution over the input elements:
* `A_softmax = softmax(A)`
4. **Weighted Sum**: Compute the weighted sum of the value vectors `V` using the attention probabilities: * `z = A_softmax * V`

Multi-Head Attention:

In practice, self-attention is often used in conjunction with multiple attention heads. This means that the input sequence is split into multiple attention heads, each with its own learnable linear transformations and attention scores. The outputs from each attention head are then concatenated and linearly transformed to produce the final output.

Benefits:

Self-attention has several benefits:

* **Parallelization**: Self-attention can be parallelized more easily thanrecurrent neural networks (RNNs), making it more efficient for long sequences.
* **Flexibility**: Self-attention can capture long-range dependencies andrelationships between input elements, making it useful for tasks like machine translation and text summarization.
* **Interpretability**: Self-attention provides a way to visualize therelationships between input elements, making it easier to understand how the model is making predictions.

Applications:

Self-attention has been widely adopted in many natural language processing (NLP) tasks, including:

* Machine translation
* Text summarization
* Sentiment analysis
* Question answering* Language modeling

It's also been used in other areas, such as computer vision and speech recognition.

Q: What metrics would you use to evaluate the performance of a multimodal model, and why are they different from traditional models?

A: Evaluating the performance of a multimodal model is more complex than traditional models because it involves multiple input or output modalities, such as text, images, audio, or video. Here are some metrics that can be used to evaluate the performance of a multimodal model, along with their differences from traditional models:

Metrics for Multimodal Models:

1.   **Multimodal Accuracy**: This metric measures the model's ability tocorrectly predict the output for a given input, considering all modalities. For example, in a visual question answering task, the model's accuracy is measured by its ability to correctly answer a question based on an image and text input.
2.   **Modal Alignment**: This metric evaluates how well the model aligns therepresentations from different modalities. For instance, in a text-image retrieval task, the model's ability to align text and image embeddings is crucial for effective retrieval.
3.   **Fusion Quality**: This metric assesses the quality of the fusion process,which combines the representations from different modalities. A good fusion process should result in a more informative and robust representation.
4.   **Modality-Specific Performance**: This metric evaluates the model'sperformance on each individual modality. For example, in a multimodal sentiment analysis task, the model's performance on text and audio modalities can be evaluated separately.
5.   **Cross-Modal Retrieval**: This metric measures the model's ability toretrieve relevant data from one modality based on a query from another modality. For example, in a text-image retrieval task, the model's ability to retrieve relevant images based on a text query is evaluated.

6.   **Multimodal Embedding Quality**: This metric evaluates the quality of the multimodal embeddings learned by the model. Good embeddings should capture the relationships between different modalities and be useful for downstream tasks.

7.   **Robustness to Missing Modalities**: This metric assesses the model's ability to perform well even when one or more modalities are missing or corrupted.

Differences from Traditional Models:

1.   **Multiple Input/Output Modalities**: Multimodal models handle multiple input or output modalities, which requires evaluating the model's performance on each modality and the interactions between them.

2.   **Modal Interactions**: Multimodal models need to capture the relationships between different modalities, which is not a concern in traditional models that focus on a single modality.

3.   **Fusion and Alignment**: Multimodal models require evaluating the quality of the fusion process and the alignment of representations from different modalities, which is not relevant in traditional models.

4.   **Increased Complexity**: Multimodal models are often more complex than traditional models, which can make evaluation more challenging due to the increased number of parameters and interactions between modalities.

5.   **Task-Specific Evaluation**: Multimodal models are often designed for specific tasks, such as visual question answering or multimodal sentiment analysis. The evaluation metrics should be tailored to the specific task and modalities involved.

In summary, evaluating the performance of a multimodal model requires considering the interactions between different modalities, the quality of the fusion process, and the model's ability to capture the relationships between modalities. The metrics used to evaluate multimodal models are often task-specific and require careful consideration of the unique characteristics of each modality and the interactions between them.

Q: Compare and contrast word embeddings and sentence embeddings. How do their applications differ, and what considerations come into play when choosing between them?

A: Word embeddings and sentence embeddings are both techniques used in natural language processing (NLP) to represent text data in a numerical format that can be processed by machine learning algorithms. While they share some similarities, they have distinct differences in their approach, applications, and use cases.

Word Embeddings:

Word embeddings, such as Word2Vec and GloVe, represent individual words as vectors in a high-dimensional space. These vectors capture the semantic meaning of words, allowing words with similar meanings to be mapped to nearby points in the vector space. Word embeddings are typically trained on large corpora of text data and are used in various NLP tasks, such as:

1. Text classification
2. Sentiment analysis
3. Named entity recognition
4. Language modeling

Sentence Embeddings:

Sentence embeddings, such as Sentence-BERT and Universal Sentence Encoder, represent entire sentences or sequences of text as vectors. These vectors capture the semantic meaning of the sentence, taking into account the context and relationships between words. Sentence embeddings are used in tasks that require a more nuanced understanding of text, such as:

1. Text similarity measurement
2. Question answering
3. Text generation
4. Dialogue systems

Comparison and Contrast:

1.   **Granularity**: Word embeddings focus on individual words, whilesentence embeddings consider the entire sentence or sequence of text.
2.   **Context**: Word embeddings capture the meaning of words in isolation,whereas sentence embeddings take into account the context in which words are used.
3.   **Dimensionality**: Word embeddings typically have lower-dimensionalvectors (e.g., 100-300 dimensions) compared to sentence embeddings (e.g., 384-768 dimensions).
4.   **Training data**: Word embeddings are often trained on large,unlabelled corpora, while sentence embeddings may require labeled data or more specialized training datasets.

Applications and Considerations:

When choosing between word embeddings and sentence embeddings, consider the following factors:

1.   **Task requirements**: If the task involves analyzing individual words orphrases, word embeddings might be sufficient. For tasks that require understanding the context and relationships between words, sentence embeddings are more suitable.
2.   **Data availability**: If labeled data is scarce, word embeddings might bea better choice. Sentence embeddings often require more data and computational resources to train.
3.   **Model complexity**: Sentence embeddings can be more computationally expensive to train and deploy, especially for longer sequences of text.
4.   **Interpretability**: Word embeddings can provide more interpretableresults, as the vectors represent individual words. Sentence embeddings can be more challenging to interpret, as the vectors represent complex semantic relationships.

Choosing between Word Embeddings and Sentence Embeddings:

1. **Use word embeddings** for tasks that involve:
* Analyzing individual words or phrases
* Working with limited computational resources
* Requiring interpretable results
2. **Use sentence embeddings** for tasks that involve:
* Understanding the context and relationships between words
* Analyzing longer sequences of text
* Requiring a more nuanced understanding of text semantics

Ultimately, the choice between word embeddings and sentence embeddings depends on the specific requirements of your project, including the task, data availability, and computational resources.

Q: Discuss common regularization techniques used during the training of embeddings to prevent overfitting and enhance the generalization ability of models.

A: Regularization Techniques for Embedding Training
===

Overfitting is a common issue in machine learning models, especially when dealing with high-dimensional data such as embeddings. Regularization techniques help prevent overfitting and improve the generalization ability of models by adding a penalty term to the loss function. Here, we'll discuss common regularization techniques used during the training of embeddings.

1. L1 and L2 Regularization

*   **L1 Regularization (Lasso Regression)**: Adds a term to the lossfunction that is proportional to the absolute value of the model's weights. This term encourages the model to set some weights to zero, effectively reducing the dimensionality of the embedding space.
*   **L2 Regularization (Ridge Regression)**: Adds a term to the lossfunction that is proportional to the square of the model's weights. This term encourages the model to reduce the magnitude of all weights, resulting in smaller embedding values.

2. Dropout

*   **Dropout**: Randomly sets a fraction of the embedding weights to zeroduring training. This technique prevents the model from relying too heavily on any single dimension and encourages it to learn more robust representations.
*   **Embedding Dropout**: A variant of dropout specifically designed forembeddings. It drops out entire embedding vectors instead of individual dimensions.
3. Early Stopping

*   **Early Stopping**: Monitors the model's performance on a validation setduring training and stops training when the performance starts to degrade. This technique prevents overfitting by stopping the training process before the model has a chance to memorize the training data.

4. Weight Decay

*   **Weight Decay**: Adds a penalty term to the loss function that isproportional to the square of the model's weights. This term encourages the model to reduce the magnitude of all weights, resulting in smaller embedding values.

5. Regularization Techniques Specific to Embeddings

*   **Orthogonality Regularization**: Encourages the embedding vectors tobe orthogonal to each other, which can help reduce the dimensionality of the embedding space and improve the model's generalization ability.   *

Normalization: Normalizes the embedding vectors to have a fixed length, which can help improve the model's stability and prevent overfitting.

Example Use Cases
----

*   **Text Classification**: Use L2 regularization to reduce the magnitude ofthe word embedding weights and prevent overfitting.
*   **Recommendation Systems**: Use dropout to prevent the model fromrelying too heavily on any single user or item embedding.
*   **Natural Language Processing**: Use early stopping to preventoverfitting when training a language model on a large corpus of text.

Best Practices
----

*   **Start with a small regularization strength**: Begin with a smallregularization strength and gradually increase it until the desired level of regularization is achieved.
*   **Monitor the model's performance**: Keep an eye on the model'sperformance on a validation set during training and adjust the regularization strength accordingly.
*   **Combine multiple regularization techniques**: Experiment withcombining multiple regularization techniques to achieve the best results.

By applying these regularization techniques, you can improve the generalization ability of your models and prevent overfitting when training embeddings. Remember to monitor the model's performance and adjust the regularization strength accordingly to achieve the best results.

Q: What is seq2seq model?

A: **Sequence-to-Sequence (Seq2Seq) Model**
=======================================

A sequence-to-sequence (seq2seq) model is a type of deep learning model used for tasks that involve generating a sequence of outputs from a sequence of inputs. This model is commonly used in natural language processing (NLP) tasks such as:

* Machine translation
* Text summarization
* Chatbots

* Dialogue systems

Architecture

The seq2seq model consists of two main components:

1.   **Encoder**: This component takes in a sequence of inputs (e.g., wordsor characters) and generates a fixed-size vector representation of the input sequence.
2.   **Decoder**: This component takes the output of the encoder andgenerates a sequence of outputs (e.g., words or characters).

The seq2seq model uses a combination of recurrent neural networks (RNNs) and attention mechanisms to generate the output sequence.

How it Works

----

1. The encoder processes the input sequence one token at a time, using aRNN (e.g., LSTM or GRU) to generate a hidden state at each time step.
2. The final hidden state of the encoder is used as the input to the decoder.
3. The decoder generates the output sequence one token at a time, using aRNN (e.g., LSTM or GRU) and an attention mechanism to focus on specific parts of the input sequence.
4. The output of the decoder at each time step is used to predict the nexttoken in the output sequence.

Types of Seq2Seq Models

There are several variants of the seq2seq model, including:

* **Basic Seq2Seq**: This is the simplest form of the seq2seq model, whichuses a single RNN for both the encoder and decoder.
* **Attention-Based Seq2Seq**: This model uses an attention mechanism tofocus on specific parts of the input sequence when generating the output sequence.
* **Bidirectional Seq2Seq**: This model uses a bidirectional RNN (e.g.,bidirectional LSTM) to process the input sequence in both the forward and backward directions.

Advantages and Disadvantages

Advantages:

* Can handle variable-length input and output sequences
* Can learn complex patterns in data* Can be used for a wide range of NLP tasks

Disadvantages:

* Can be computationally expensive to train
* Can suffer from vanishing gradients and exploding gradients
* Can require large amounts of training data to achieve good performance

Example Use Case

A seq2seq model can be used to build a machine translation system that translates English text to Spanish text. The input sequence would be the English text, and the output sequence would be the Spanish text. The seq2seq model would learn to generate the Spanish translation based on the input English text.

Q: What are Transformers?

A: Transformers are a type of neural network architecture introduced in the paper "Attention Is All You Need" by Vaswani et al. in 2017. They revolutionized the field of natural language processing (NLP) and have since been widely adopted in various AI applications.

Key Characteristics:

1.   **Self-Attention Mechanism**: Transformers rely on self-attention, whichallows the model to weigh the importance of different input elements (e.g., words or tokens) relative to each other. This enables the model to capture long-range dependencies and contextual relationships.
2.   **Encoder-Decoder Architecture**: Transformers consist of an encoderand a decoder. The encoder takes in a sequence of input elements and generates a continuous representation of the input. The decoder then generates the output sequence, one element at a time, based on the encoder's output.
3.   **No Recurrence or Convolution**: Unlike traditional recurrent neuralnetworks (RNNs) or convolutional neural networks (CNNs), Transformers do not use recurrence or convolution to process input sequences. Instead, they rely on self-attention and feed-forward neural networks (FFNNs).

How Transformers Work:

1.   **Input Embeddings**: The input sequence is embedded into a vectorspace using an embedding layer.
2.   **Encoder**: The embedded input is fed into the encoder, which consistsof a series of identical layers. Each layer applies self-attention, followed by an FFNN.
3.   **Self-Attention**:   The   self-attention   mechanism   computes   the weightedsum of the input elements, where the weights are learned based on the input elements' relationships.
4.   **Decoder**: The decoder generates the output sequence, one elementat a time, based on the encoder's output. The decoder also consists of a series of identical layers, each applying self-attention, followed by an FFNN.
5.   **Output**: The final output is generated by taking the output of thedecoder and applying a softmax layer to obtain a probability distribution over the possible output elements.

Advantages:

1.   **Parallelization**: Transformers can be parallelized more easily thanRNNs, making them faster to train and more efficient.
2.   **Scalability**: Transformers can handle longer input sequences andlarger models than RNNs.
3.   **Performance**: Transformers have achieved state-of-the-art results inmany NLP tasks, such as machine translation, text classification, and question answering.

Applications:

1.   **Machine Translation**: Transformers have been used to improvemachine translation systems, such as Google Translate.
2.   **Text Classification**: Transformers have been used for textclassification tasks, such as sentiment analysis and spam detection.
3.   **Question Answering**: Transformers have been used to improvequestion answering systems, such as those used in chatbots and virtual assistants.

In summary, Transformers are a type of neural network architecture that relies on self-attention and feed-forward neural networks to process input sequences. They have revolutionized the field of NLP and have many applications in AI, including machine translation, text classification, and question answering.

Q: What is Attention? What are some attention mechanism types?

A: **Attention** is a concept in deep learning that allows models to focus on specific parts of the input data when making predictions. It's inspired by the way humans pay attention to certain aspects of their environment while ignoring others. In the context of neural networks, attention mechanisms enable the model to weigh the importance of different input elements, such as words in a sentence or pixels in an image, when generating output.

Types of Attention Mechanisms:

1.   **Scaled Dot-Product Attention**: This is a widely used attentionmechanism introduced in the Transformer model. It calculates the attention weights by taking the dot product of the query and key vectors and applying a softmax function.

2.   **Multi-Head Attention**: This is an extension of scaled dot-productattention, where the model uses multiple attention heads to jointly attend to information from different representation subspaces.

3.   **Self-Attention**: This type of attention allows the model to attend todifferent parts of the input sequence itself, such as attending to different words in a sentence.

4.   **Hierarchical Attention**: This attention mechanism is used in modelsthat process hierarchical data, such as sentences or documents. It allows the model to attend to different levels of the hierarchy, such as attending to sentences or paragraphs.

5.   **Local Attention**: This attention mechanism focuses on a specific partof the input data, such as a local region in an image.

6.   **Global Attention**: This attention mechanism considers the entire inputdata when calculating attention weights.

7.   **Hard Attention**: This type of attention uses a binary mask to select asubset of the input data to focus on.

8.   **Soft Attention**: This type of attention uses a continuous weightdistribution to focus on different parts of the input data.

Applications of Attention Mechanisms:

1.   **Natural Language Processing (NLP)**: Attention mechanisms arewidely used in NLP tasks, such as machine translation, text summarization, and question answering.

2.   **Computer Vision**: Attention mechanisms are used in computer visiontasks, such as image captioning, object detection, and image segmentation.

3.   **Speech Recognition**: Attention mechanisms are used in speechrecognition tasks to focus on specific parts of the audio signal.

Benefits of Attention Mechanisms:

1. **Improved Performance**: Attention mechanisms can improve theperformance of models by allowing them to focus on the most relevant parts of the input data.
2. **Interpretability**: Attention mechanisms can provide insights into whichparts of the input data are most important for the model's predictions.
3. **Efficiency**: Attention mechanisms can reduce the computationalrequirements of models by allowing them to focus on a subset of the input data.

Q: What are different Prompting techniques?

A: There are several prompting techniques used to elicit specific responses or guide the conversation in a desired direction. Here are some common ones:

1. **Open-Ended Prompts**: These encourage the respondent to sharetheir thoughts, feelings, or experiences in detail. Examples: "Can you tell me more about...", "How did you feel about...", or "What was your experience like...".

2. **Closed-Ended Prompts**: These are used to gather specific, factualinformation and typically result in a brief response. Examples: "What is your name?", "How old are you?", or "Do you like...".

3. **Probing Prompts**: These are used to gather more information orclarify a response. Examples: "Can you elaborate on that?", "What do you mean by...", or "How did that make you feel?".

4. **Reflective Prompts**: These involve mirroring or reflecting therespondent's words or emotions to show understanding and encourage further discussion. Examples: "Just to make sure I understand, you're saying...", "I sense that you're feeling...", or "It sounds like...".

5. **Leading Prompts**: These are used to guide the respondent towards aspecific response or topic. Examples: "Don't you think that...", "Isn't it true that...", or "Wouldn't you agree that...".

6. **Funneling Prompts**: These start with open-ended questions andgradually become more specific to gather detailed information. Examples: "What do you think about...?" (open-ended) -> "What specific aspects of... do you like?" (more specific) -> "Can you give me an example of...?" (very specific).

7.   **Scaling Prompts**: These ask the respondent to rate their feelings oropinions on a scale. Examples: "On a scale of 1-10, how would you rate...", "How satisfied are you with...?" (very satisfied, somewhat satisfied, etc.), or "How likely are you to...?" (very likely, somewhat likely, etc.).

8.   **Emotional Prompts**: These are used to explore the respondent'semotions and feelings. Examples: "How did that make you feel?", "What emotions did you experience during...", or "Can you describe your emotional state when...".

9.   **Hypothetical Prompts**: These present a hypothetical scenario togather information about the respondent's thoughts, feelings, or behaviors in a specific situation. Examples: "What would you do if...", "How would you feel if...", or "What would you think if...".

10.   **Storytelling Prompts**: These encourage the respondent to share apersonal story or anecdote. Examples: "Can you tell me a story about...", "What's a memorable experience you've had with...", or "How did you first get interested in...".

These prompting techniques can be used in various contexts, such as interviews, surveys, focus groups, or even everyday conversations.

Q: What is PEFT LoRA in Fine tuning?

A: PEFT (Parameter-Efficient Fine-Tuning) and LoRA (Low-Rank Adaptation) are both techniques used in fine-tuning pre-trained language models, particularly in the context of transformer-based architectures.

PEFT:
Parameter-Efficient Fine-Tuning (PEFT) is a family of methods that aim to reduce the number of parameters that need to be updated during fine-tuning. The idea is to freeze most of the pre-trained model's weights and only update a small subset of parameters, typically the weights of the output layer or a few intermediate layers. This approach is motivated by the observation that pre-trained models often have a large number of redundant parameters, and fine-tuning only a small subset of them can be sufficient to adapt the model to a new task.

LoRA:
Low-Rank Adaptation (LoRA) is a specific technique for fine-tuning pre-trained models that is based on the idea of low-rank matrix approximation. The basic idea is to represent the weight updates as a low-rank matrix, which can be factorized into two

smaller matrices. This allows for a significant reduction in the number of parameters that need to be updated, making the fine-tuning process more efficient.

In the context of fine-tuning, LoRA can be seen as a way to adapt the pre-trained model's weights by adding a low-rank update matrix to the original weights. This update matrix is learned during fine-tuning and is typically much smaller than the original weight matrix.

PEFT-LoRA:
PEFT-LoRA is a specific implementation that combines the ideas of PEFT and LoRA. In this approach, the pre-trained model's weights are frozen, and a low-rank update matrix is learned using the LoRA technique. The update matrix is then added to the original weights to adapt the model to the new task. This approach has been shown to be highly effective in fine-tuning pre-trained models, particularly in low-resource settings where the amount of training data is limited.

Overall, PEFT-LoRA is a powerful technique for fine-tuning pre-trained models, as it allows for efficient adaptation to new tasks while minimizing the number of parameters that need to be updated. This can lead to significant improvements in performance, particularly in low-resource settings.

Q: What are the key challenges in indexing and searching through high-dimensional vector spaces?

A: Indexing and searching through high-dimensional vector spaces pose several key challenges:

1.   **Curse of Dimensionality**: As the number of dimensions increases, thevolume of the space grows exponentially, making it difficult to efficiently search and index the data. This leads to a decrease in search performance and an increase in storage requirements.

2.   **Distance Metric Degradation**: Traditional distance metrics, such asEuclidean distance, become less effective in high-dimensional spaces. This is because the distances between points become more similar, making it harder to distinguish between similar and dissimilar points.

3.   **Indexing Complexity**: High-dimensional data requires complexindexing structures, such as trees or graphs, to efficiently store and retrieve data. However, these structures can become cumbersome to manage and update, especially for large datasets.

4. **Scalability**: High-dimensional data often requires significant storageand computational resources, making it challenging to scale indexing and search systems to handle large datasets.

5. **Query Performance**: Searching through high-dimensional spaces canbe computationally expensive, leading to slow query performance and long response times.

6. **Data Sparsity**: High-dimensional data often suffers from the "sparsity"problem, where most of the dimensions are irrelevant or contain little information. This can lead to poor search performance and decreased accuracy.

7. **Noise and Outliers**: High-dimensional data can be noisy and containoutliers, which can negatively impact search performance and accuracy.

8. **Dimensionality Reduction**: Reducing the dimensionality of the datawhile preserving its meaningful structure and relationships is a challenging task, especially when dealing with high-dimensional data.

9. **Approximation Techniques**: Approximation techniques, such ashashing or quantization, can be used to reduce the dimensionality and improve search performance. However, these techniques can also lead to a loss of accuracy and precision.

10. **Evaluation Metrics**: Evaluating the performance of indexing andsearch systems in high-dimensional spaces can be challenging due to the lack of clear evaluation metrics and benchmarks.

To overcome these challenges, various techniques and algorithms have been developed, such as:

* **Approximate Nearest Neighbors (ANN)**: algorithms that useapproximation techniques to quickly find nearest neighbors in high-dimensional spaces.

* **Hashing-based indexing**: techniques that use hash functions to maphigh-dimensional data to lower-dimensional spaces.

* **Dimensionality reduction**: techniques, such as PCA or t-SNE, thatreduce the dimensionality of the data while preserving its meaningful structure and relationships.

* **Graph-based indexing**: techniques that use graph structures toefficiently store and retrieve high-dimensional data.

* **Distributed indexing**: techniques that distribute the indexing and searchprocess across multiple machines or nodes to improve scalability and performance.

These techniques and algorithms have been successfully applied in various domains, such as computer vision, natural language processing, and recommender systems, to efficiently index and search through high-dimensional vector spaces.

Q: How can you handle vector data that may have different dimensionalities or representations?

A: Handling Vector Data with Different Dimensionalities or Representations

===
===========

Vector data can come in various forms, such as different dimensionalities or representations. To handle these variations, you can use the following approaches:

1. **Data Normalization**

Normalize the vector data to a common scale, usually between 0 and 1, to ensure that all features are on the same scale. This can be done using techniques such as:

*   Min-Max Scaling
*   Standardization (mean = 0, standard deviation = 1)* Log Scaling

2. **Dimensionality Reduction**

Reduce the dimensionality of high-dimensional vector data to a lower-dimensional representation using techniques such as:

*   Principal Component Analysis (PCA)
*   t-Distributed Stochastic Neighbor Embedding (t-SNE)* Autoencoders

3. **Feature Extraction**

Extract relevant features from the vector data, such as:

*   Using Fourier Transform to extract frequency features
*   Using Wavelet Transform to extract time-frequency features
*   Using convolutional neural networks to extract spatial features

4. **Data Augmentation**

Augment the vector data to increase its size and diversity, such as:

* Adding noise to the data
* Rotating or flipping the data
* Generating new data using Generative Adversarial Networks (GANs)

5. **Using Robust Algorithms**

Use algorithms that are robust to variations in dimensionality or representation, such as:

* Using k-Nearest Neighbors (k-NN) algorithm, which can handlehigh-dimensional data
* Using Support Vector Machines (SVMs), which can handle high-dimensional data and non-linear relationships

Example Use Case: Handling Vector Data with Different Dimensionalities

----

Suppose we have a dataset of images with different resolutions (e.g., 256x256, 512x512, etc.). We can use the following approach to handle the different dimensionalities:

* Normalize the images to a common scale using Min-Max Scaling
* Reduce the dimensionality of the images using PCA
* Extract relevant features from the images using convolutional neuralnetworks
* Use a robust algorithm such as k-NN or SVM to classify the images

Code Example: Handling Vector Data with Different Dimensionalities

----

```python
import numpy as np
from sklearn.preprocessing import MinMaxScaler from
sklearn.decomposition import PCA from
sklearn.neighbors import KNeighborsClassifier from
sklearn.metrics import accuracy_score

# Load the dataset
X_train = np.random.rand(100, 256*256)  # 100 images with 256x256 resolution
y_train = np.random.randint(0, 2, 100)  # 100 labels

X_test = np.random.rand(20, 512*512) # 20 images with 512x512 resolution
```

```
y_test = np.random.randint(0, 2, 20) # 20 labels

# Normalize the data scaler =
MinMaxScaler()
X_train_scaled = scaler.fit_transform(X_train) X_test_scaled =
scaler.transform(X_test)

# Reduce the dimensionality of the data pca =
PCA(n_components=128)
X_train_pca = pca.fit_transform(X_train_scaled) X_test_pca =
pca.transform(X_test_scaled)

# Train a k-NN classifier
knn = KNeighborsClassifier(n_neighbors=5)    knn.fit(X_train_pca,
y_train)
# Evaluate the classifier y_pred =
knn.predict(X_test_pca) accuracy =
accuracy_score(y_test, y_pred)
print("Accuracy:", accuracy)
```
```

In this example, we normalize the images to a common scale using Min-Max Scaling, reduce the dimensionality of the images using PCA, and train a k-NN classifier to classify the images. The classifier is robust to variations in dimensionality and can handle high-dimensional data.

## Q: What is model or concept drift?

A: Model or concept drift refers to the phenomenon where the underlying relationships or patterns in the data used to train a machine learning model change over time. This change can cause the model's performance to degrade, as it is no longer accurately representing the current data distribution.

Concept drift can occur due to various reasons, such as:

1.     **Changes in user behavior**: User preferences, habits, or behaviorsmay change over time, affecting the data distribution.
2.     **Seasonality**: Seasonal patterns can cause changes in datadistributions, such as increased sales during holidays or summer months.
3.     **New trends or events**: Emergence of new trends, technologies, orevents can shift the data distribution.
```

4.   **Data quality issues**: Changes in data collection methods,instrumentation, or measurement tools can introduce biases or errors.

5.   **Concept evolution**: The underlying concept or definition of a variablemay change over time, such as changes in medical diagnosis criteria.

Types of concept drift:

1. **Sudden drift**: Abrupt changes in the data distribution.
2. **Gradual drift**: Slow, continuous changes in the data distribution.
3. **Recurring drift**: Periodic changes in the data distribution, such asseasonal patterns.

To address concept drift, various strategies can be employed, including:

1.   **Model updating**: Re-training the model on new data to adapt tochanges.
2.   **Online learning**: Updating the model in real-time as new data arrives.3. **Ensemble methods**: Combining multiple models to improve robustness to concept drift.
4. **Active learning**: Selectively sampling new data to update the model.
5. **Drift detection**: Monitoring the data distribution for changes andtriggering model updates when necessary.

By acknowledging and addressing concept drift, machine learning models can maintain their performance and accuracy over time, ensuring reliable and effective decision-making.

Q: How do you implement model monitoring in a production environment?

A: Implementing model monitoring in a production environment is crucial to ensure that machine learning models continue to perform well and make accurate predictions over time. Here's a step-by-step guide on how to implement model monitoring:

1.   **Define Monitoring Metrics**: Identify the key performance indicators(KPIs) that will be used to evaluate the model's performance. These metrics may include accuracy, precision, recall, F1 score, mean squared error, or other relevant metrics.

2.   **Data Ingestion**: Set up a data pipeline to collect and store data fromthe production environment. This data will be used to monitor the model's performance and detect any issues.

3.   **Model Serving**: Deploy the model in a production-ready environment,such as a cloud-based platform or a containerized application.

4.   **Monitoring Dashboard**: Create a monitoring dashboard to visualizethe model's performance metrics and KPIs. This dashboard should provide real-time insights into the model's performance and allow for easy identification of issues.

5.   **Data Quality Checks**: Implement data quality checks to ensure thatthe data being used to monitor the model is accurate and consistent. This includes checks for missing values, outliers, and data distribution shifts.

6.   **Model Performance Tracking**: Track the model's performance overtime, using metrics such as accuracy, precision, and recall. This will help identify any changes in the model's performance and allow for prompt intervention if necessary.

7.   **Drift Detection**: Implement drift detection algorithms to identifychanges in the data distribution or concept drift. This will help detect issues such as data quality problems, changes in user behavior, or external factors that may affect the model's performance.

8.   **Alerting and Notification**: Set up alerting and notification systems tonotify teams when issues are detected. This may include email notifications, SMS alerts, or integration with incident management tools.

9.   **Model Updates and Retraining**: Develop a process for updating andretraining the model as needed. This may involve retraining the model on new data, updating the model architecture, or adjusting hyperparameters. 10. **Continuous Integration and Continuous Deployment (CI/CD)**: Implement a CI/CD pipeline to automate the deployment of updated models and ensure that changes are properly tested and validated before being deployed to production.

Tools and Technologies:

1.   **Monitoring Platforms**: Use monitoring platforms such as Prometheus,Grafana, or New Relic to collect and visualize metrics.

2.   **Model Serving Platforms**: Use model serving platforms such asTensorFlow Serving, AWS SageMaker, or Azure Machine Learning to deploy and manage models.

3.   **Data Quality Tools**: Use data quality tools such as Great Expectationsor Apache Beam to implement data quality checks.

4.   **Drift Detection Libraries**: Use drift detection libraries such asscikit-learn or statsmodels to implement drift detection algorithms.

5.   **CI/CD Tools**: Use CI/CD tools such as Jenkins, GitLab CI/CD, orCircleCI to automate the deployment of updated models.

Best Practices:

1.   **Monitor Multiple Metrics**: Monitor multiple metrics to get acomprehensive view of the model's performance.

2.   **Use Real-time Data**: Use real-time data to monitor the model'sperformance and detect issues promptly.

3.   **Implement Automated Testing**: Implement automated testing toensure that changes to the model or data pipeline do not introduce issues.

4.   **Use Version Control**: Use version control to track changes to themodel and data pipeline.

5.   **Continuously Evaluate and Improve**: Continuously evaluate andimprove the model monitoring process to ensure that it is effective and efficient.

Q: Suppose your deployed model's performance suddenly drops. What steps would you take to diagnose and resolve the issue?

A: **Diagnosing and Resolving Sudden Performance Drop in a Deployed Model**

Step 1: Gather Information

*   **Monitor logs**: Check the model's logs to identify any error messages,warnings, or unusual patterns that may indicate the cause of the performance drop.
*   **Collect metrics**: Gather relevant metrics, such as accuracy, precision,recall, F1 score, and latency, to quantify the performance drop.
*   **Data inspection**: Inspect the input data to ensure it is consistent withthe training data and meets the expected quality standards.

Step 2: Analyze the Data

*   **Data distribution shift**: Check if there has been a significant change inthe data distribution, such as a shift in the input data's mean, variance, or correlation structure.
*   **Data quality issues**: Investigate if there are any data quality issues,such as missing values, outliers, or noisy data, that may be affecting the model's performance.
*   **Concept drift**: Determine if the underlying concept or relationshipbetween the input data and target variable has changed over time.

Step 3: Model Analysis

*   **Model degradation**: Check if the model has degraded over time due tofactors such as overfitting, underfitting, or changes in the data distribution. *

Model updates: Verify if any recent model updates, such as changes to the architecture, hyperparameters, or training data, may have caused the performance drop.

* **Model interpretability**: Use techniques such as feature importance, partial dependence plots, and SHAP values to understand how the model is making predictions and identify potential issues.

Step 4: Troubleshooting

* **Re-train the model**: Re-train the model using the latest data to ensure it is adapted to any changes in the data distribution or concept drift.
* **Hyperparameter tuning**: Perform hyperparameter tuning to optimize the model's performance on the current data.
* **Model selection**: Consider alternative models or architectures that may be more robust to changes in the data distribution or concept drift.

Step 5: Resolution and Monitoring

* **Implement fixes**: Implement any necessary fixes, such as data preprocessing changes, model updates, or hyperparameter tuning.
* **Monitor performance**: Continuously monitor the model's performance to ensure the fixes have resolved the issue and to detect any future performance drops.
* **Automated monitoring**: Set up automated monitoring and alerting systems to quickly detect and respond to any future performance issues.

Example Code (Python)
```python
import pandas as pd
from sklearn.metrics import accuracy_score, classification_report, confusion_matrix
from sklearn.model_selection import train_test_split
from sklearn.ensemble import RandomForestClassifier
from sklearn.model_selection import GridSearchCV

# Load data
df = pd.read_csv('data.csv')

# Split data into training and testing sets
X_train, X_test, y_train, y_test = train_test_split(df.drop('target', axis=1), df['target'], test_size=0.2, random_state=42)
```

```
# Train model
model   =   RandomForestClassifier()   model.fit(X_train,
y_train)

# Evaluate model performance y_pred =
model.predict(X_test)
print('Accuracy:', accuracy_score(y_test, y_pred))
print('Classification Report:')
print(classification_report(y_test,   y_pred))   print('Confusion
Matrix:')
print(confusion_matrix(y_test, y_pred))

# Perform hyperparameter tuning
param_grid = {'n_estimators': [100, 200, 300], 'max_depth': [5, 10, 15]} grid_search
= GridSearchCV(model, param_grid, cv=5, scoring='accuracy')
grid_search.fit(X_train, y_train)

# Print best hyperparameters and re-train model print('Best
Hyperparameters:', grid_search.best_params_) best_model =
grid_search.best_estimator_
best_model.fit(X_train, y_train)
```
```

This code snippet demonstrates how to load data, split it into training and testing sets, train a model, evaluate its performance, and perform hyperparameter tuning using GridSearchCV.
```

Machine Learning

Q: What is regularization in machine learning, State the differences between L1 and L2 regularization

A: **Regularization in Machine Learning**
==

Regularization is a technique used in machine learning to prevent overfitting by adding a penalty term to the loss function. Overfitting occurs when a model is too complex and performs well on the training data but poorly on new, unseen data. Regularization helps to reduce the complexity of the model by adding a term to the loss function that discourages large weights.

Types of Regularization

There are two main types of regularization: L1 and L2 regularization.

L1 Regularization (Lasso Regression)

*   **Definition:** L1 regularization, also known as Lasso regression, adds aterm to the loss function that is proportional to the absolute value of the model's weights.
*   **Mathematical Formula:** `Loss = Error + ? * ?|w_i|`
*   **Effect:** L1 regularization sets some model weights to zero, effectivelyremoving the corresponding features from the model. This is known as feature selection.
*   **Use Cases:** L1 regularization is useful when you want to performfeature selection or when you have a large number of features and want to reduce the dimensionality of the data.

L2 Regularization (Ridge Regression)

*   **Definition:** L2 regularization, also known as Ridge regression, adds aterm to the loss function that is proportional to the square of the model's weights.
*   **Mathematical Formula:** `Loss = Error + ? * ?w_i^2`
*   **Effect:** L2 regularization reduces the magnitude of all model weights,but does not set any weights to zero. This is known as weight decay. *   **Use Cases:** L2 regularization is useful when you want to reduce the impact of overfitting without removing any features from the model.

Key Differences
----

* **Feature Selection:** L1 regularization performs feature selection by setting some model weights to zero, while L2 regularization does not.
* **Weight Reduction:** L2 regularization reduces the magnitude of all model weights, while L1 regularization reduces the magnitude of some model weights to zero.
* **Effect on Model Complexity:** L1 regularization can reduce the model complexity by removing features, while L2 regularization reduces the model complexity by reducing the magnitude of the weights.

Example Use Case

Suppose you are building a linear regression model to predict house prices based on features such as number of bedrooms, square footage, and location. You have a large number of features and want to reduce the dimensionality of the data. In this case, you would use L1 regularization to perform feature selection and reduce the number of features in the model.

On the other hand, if you want to reduce the impact of overfitting without removing any features from the model, you would use L2 regularization.

Code Example (Python)
```python
import numpy as np
from sklearn.linear_model import Lasso, Ridge from
sklearn.datasets import make_regression from
sklearn.model_selection import train_test_split

# Generate sample data
X, y = make_regression(n_samples=100, n_features=10, noise=0.1)

# Split data into training and testing sets
X_train, X_test, y_train, y_test = train_test_split(X, y, test_size=0.2)

# L1 Regularization (Lasso Regression) lasso_model =
Lasso(alpha=0.1) lasso_model.fit(X_train, y_train)

# L2 Regularization (Ridge Regression) ridge_model =
Ridge(alpha=0.1) ridge_model.fit(X_train, y_train)

# Print coefficients
```

```
print("Lasso    Coefficients:",    lasso_model.coef_)    print("Ridge
Coefficients:", ridge_model.coef_)
```
```

In this example, we use the `Lasso` and `Ridge` classes from scikit-learn to implement L1 and L2 regularization, respectively. We then print the coefficients of the models to see the effect of regularization on the model weights.

## Q: Explain the concepts of bias-variance trade-off in machine learning.

A: The bias-variance trade-off is a fundamental concept in machine learning that refers to the inherent trade-off between the accuracy and complexity of a model. It is a crucial aspect of model selection, regularization, and hyperparameter tuning.

**What is Bias?**

Bias refers to the error introduced by a model due to its simplifying assumptions or limitations. A model with high bias pays little attention to the training data and oversimplifies the relationship between the input and output variables. As a result, the model fails to capture the underlying patterns in the data, leading to poor predictions.

**What is Variance?**

Variance, on the other hand, refers to the error introduced by a model due to its sensitivity to the training data. A model with high variance is overly complex and fits the training data too closely, including the noise and random fluctuations. This results in poor generalization performance, as the model is not able to make accurate predictions on new, unseen data.

**The Trade-off**

The bias-variance trade-off arises because a model that is too simple (high bias) will not capture the underlying patterns in the data, while a model that is too complex (high variance) will overfit the training data. The ideal model should strike a balance between these two extremes, achieving a good trade-off between bias and variance.
**Key Concepts**

1.      **Underfitting**: A model with high bias that fails to capture theunderlying patterns in the data.
2.      **Overfitting**: A model with high variance that fits the training data tooclosely, including the noise and random fluctuations.
```

3.   **Optimal Model**: A model that achieves a good balance between biasand variance, resulting in the best possible performance on both the training and test data.

Factors that Affect the Bias-Variance Trade-off

1.   **Model Complexity**: Increasing the complexity of a model can reducebias but increase variance.
2.   **Training Data Size**: Increasing the size of the training data can reducevariance but may not affect bias.
3.   **Regularization**: Regularization techniques, such as L1 and L2 regularization, can reduce variance by adding a penalty term to the loss function.
4.   **Hyperparameter Tuning**: Hyperparameter tuning can help find theoptimal balance between bias and variance.

Techniques to Address the Bias-Variance Trade-off

1.   **Cross-Validation**: Splitting the data into training and test sets toevaluate the model's performance.
2.   **Regularization**: Using techniques such as L1 and L2 regularization toreduce variance.
3.   **Early Stopping**: Stopping the training process when the model'sperformance on the validation set starts to degrade.
4.   **Ensemble Methods**: Combining multiple models to reduce varianceand improve overall performance.

In summary, the bias-variance trade-off is a fundamental concept in machine learning that highlights the importance of finding a balance between model complexity and generalization performance. By understanding the factors that affect this trade-off and using techniques to address it, machine learning practitioners can develop more accurate and robust models.

Q: How we will deal with the categorical text values in machine learning?

A: Dealing with categorical text values is a common challenge in machine learning. Here are some ways to handle categorical text values:

1.   **Label Encoding**: This involves assigning a numerical value to eachcategory. For example, if we have a column with categories "yes", "no", and "maybe", we can assign 0, 1, and 2 to each category respectively. However, this

method can be problematic if the model interprets the numerical values as having a specific order or magnitude.

2.   **One-Hot Encoding (OHE)**: This involves creating a new binarycolumn for each category. For example, if we have a column with categories "yes", "no", and "maybe", we can create three new columns: "yes", "no", and "maybe", where each column has a value of 1 if the original column has that category and 0 otherwise. This method is more robust than label encoding but can result in a large number of new columns.

3.   **Binary Encoding**: This involves converting each category into a binaryvector. For example, if we have a column with categories "yes", "no", and "maybe", we can convert each category into a binary vector: "yes" = [1, 0, 0], "no" = [0, 1, 0], and "maybe" = [0, 0, 1].

4.   **Hashing**: This involves using a hash function to convert eachcategory into a numerical value. For example, we can use the `hash()` function in Python to convert each category into a numerical value.

5.   **Target Encoding**: This involves encoding the categorical variablesbased on the target variable. For example, if we have a column with categories "yes", "no", and "maybe", and a target variable "response", we can calculate the mean response for each category and use that as the encoded value.

6.   **Word Embeddings**: This involves using word embeddings likeWord2Vec or GloVe to convert text data into numerical vectors. This method is particularly useful for natural language processing tasks.

7.   **Ordinal Encoding**: This involves encoding categorical variables thathave a natural order or ranking. For example, if we have a column with categories "low", "medium", and "high", we can assign 1, 2, and 3 to each category respectively.

When to use each method:

*   Use label encoding when the categorical variable has a small number ofcategories and the model can handle numerical values.

*   Use one-hot encoding when the categorical variable has a large numberof categories and the model can handle binary values.

*   Use binary encoding when the categorical variable has a large number ofcategories and the model can handle binary vectors.

*   Use hashing when the categorical variable has a large number ofcategories and the model can handle numerical values.

*   Use target encoding when the categorical variable is highly correlated withthe target variable.

*   Use word embeddings when working with text data and the model canhandle numerical vectors.

*   Use ordinal encoding when the categorical variable has a natural order orranking.

Example code:

. Here is an example of how to use one-hot encoding in Python using the `pandas` library: ```python import pandas as pd

# create a sample dataframe
df = pd.DataFrame({'category': ['yes', 'no', 'maybe', 'yes', 'no']})

one-hot encode the category column df_ohe = pd.get_dummies(df, columns=['category'])

print(df_ohe)
```

This will output:
```

   category_no category_maybe category_yes
0   0   0   1
1   1   0   0
2   0   1   0
3   0   0   1
4   1   0   0
```

Note that the `get_dummies()` function creates new columns for each category and assigns a value of 1 if the original column has that category and 0 otherwise.

## Q: What is the cross-validation technique in machine learning?

A: Cross-validation is a technique used in machine learning to evaluate the performance of a model on unseen data. It's a way to assess how well a model will generalize to new, unseen data, by training and testing the model on multiple subsets of the available data.

**Why is cross-validation needed?**

When you train a model on a dataset, it may perform well on that specific dataset, but it may not generalize well to new, unseen data. This is known as overfitting. Cross-validation helps to mitigate overfitting by evaluating the model's performance on multiple subsets of the data, rather than just the training data.

**How does cross-validation work?**
```

Here are the general steps involved in cross-validation:

1.   **Split the data**: Divide the available dataset into two parts: a trainingset and a test set.
2.   **Split the training set**: Further divide the training set into multiplesubsets, called folds.
3.   **Train and test**: Train the model on one fold and test it on theremaining folds.
4.   **Repeat**: Repeat steps 3 for each fold, so that each fold is used as atest set once.
5.   **Evaluate**:   Calculate   the   performance   metric   (e.g.,   accuracy, precision,recall) for each test set.
6.   **Average**: Calculate the average performance metric across all testsets.

Types of cross-validation

There are several types of cross-validation techniques, including:

1.   **K-fold cross-validation**: This is the most common type, where the datais split into k folds, and the model is trained and tested on each fold.
2.   **Leave-one-out   cross-validation**:   This   type   of   cross-validation involvestraining the model on all but one sample, and then testing it on that sample. This process is repeated for each sample in the dataset.
3.   **Stratified cross-validation**: This type of cross-validation is used whenthe dataset is imbalanced, and the model needs to be evaluated on each class separately.

Advantages of cross-validation

1.   **Reduces overfitting**: Cross-validation helps to prevent overfitting byevaluating the model on multiple subsets of the data.
2.   **Improves model selection**: Cross-validation helps to select the bestmodel for a given problem by evaluating the performance of different models on the same dataset.
3.   **Provides a more accurate estimate**: Cross-validation provides a moreaccurate estimate of the model's performance on unseen data.

Common applications of cross-validation

1.   **Model selection**: Cross-validation is used to select the best model fora given problem.

2.   **Hyperparameter tuning**: Cross-validation is used to tune thehyperparameters of a model.

3.   **Model evaluation**: Cross-validation is used to evaluate theperformance of a model on unseen data.

In summary, cross-validation is a powerful technique used in machine learning to evaluate the performance of a model on unseen data. It helps to reduce overfitting, improve model selection, and provide a more accurate estimate of the model's performance.

Q: Describe gradient descent and its role in optimizing machine learning models.

A: **Gradient Descent: A Fundamental Optimization Algorithm in Machine Learning**
===
===========

Gradient descent is a widely used optimization algorithm in machine learning that plays a crucial role in training and fine-tuning models. In this response, we will delve into the concept of gradient descent, its types, and its significance in optimizing machine learning models.

What is Gradient Descent?

Gradient descent is an iterative algorithm that minimizes the loss function of a machine learning model by adjusting its parameters in the direction of the negative gradient of the loss function. The goal is to find the optimal values of the model's parameters that result in the minimum loss.

How Gradient Descent Works

The gradient descent algorithm works as follows:

1.   **Initialize parameters**: The model's parameters are initialized withrandom or predefined values.

2.   **Compute loss**: The loss function is computed using the currentparameters and the training data.

3.   **Compute gradient**: The gradient of the loss function with respect toeach parameter is computed using backpropagation.

4.   **Update parameters**: The parameters are updated by subtracting theproduct of the learning rate and the gradient from the current parameters.

5.   **Repeat**: Steps 2-4 are repeated until convergence or a stoppingcriterion is reached.

Types of Gradient Descent

There are several variants of gradient descent, including:

*   **Batch Gradient Descent**: The gradient is computed using the entiretraining dataset.
*   **Stochastic Gradient Descent (SGD)**: The gradient is computed using asingle example from the training dataset.
*   **Mini-Batch Gradient Descent**: The gradient is computed using a smallbatch of examples from the training dataset.
*   **Momentum Gradient Descent**: The update rule includes a momentumterm that helps escape local minima.
*   **Nesterov Accelerated Gradient (NAG)**: A variant of momentumgradient descent that incorporates a correction term.

Role in Optimizing Machine Learning Models

Gradient descent plays a vital role in optimizing machine learning models by:

*   **Minimizing loss**: Gradient descent minimizes the loss function, which isa measure of the difference between the model's predictions and the actual labels.
*   **Improving accuracy**: By minimizing the loss, gradient descentimproves the model's accuracy and performance on the training data. * **Regularization**: Gradient descent can be used to regularize the model by adding a penalty term to the loss function, which helps prevent overfitting.
*   **Hyperparameter tuning**: Gradient descent can be used to tunehyperparameters, such as the learning rate and regularization strength, to optimize the model's performance.

Example Use Case

Suppose we want to train a linear regression model to predict house prices based on features such as number of bedrooms, square footage, and location. We can use gradient descent to optimize the model's parameters (weights and bias) to minimize the mean squared error between the predicted prices and the actual prices.

```python
import numpy as np

# Define the loss function
def loss(y_pred, y_true):
    return np.mean((y_pred - y_true) ** 2)

# Define the gradient descent update rule
def update_params(params, learning_rate, gradient):
    return params - learning_rate * gradient

# Initialize parameters
weights = np.random.rand(3)
bias = np.random.rand(1)

# Define the training data
X = np.array([[1, 2, 3], [4, 5, 6], [7, 8, 9]])
y = np.array([10, 20, 30])

# Train the model using gradient descent
for i in range(1000):
    # Compute predictions
    y_pred = np.dot(X, weights) + bias

    # Compute loss
    loss_value = loss(y_pred, y)

    # Compute gradient
    gradient = np.dot(X.T, (y_pred - y)) / len(y)

    # Update parameters
    weights = update_params(weights, 0.01, gradient)
    bias = update_params(bias, 0.01, np.mean(y_pred - y))

    # Print loss
    print(f'Loss at iteration {i}: {loss_value}')
```

In conclusion, gradient descent is a fundamental optimization algorithm in machine learning that plays a crucial role in training and fine-tuning models. Its variants and applications make it a versatile tool for optimizing machine learning models.

Q: What is the difference between MLOps and DevOps?

A: MLOps (Machine Learning Operations) and DevOps (Development Operations) are two related but distinct disciplines that aim to improve the efficiency and reliability of software development and deployment. The main difference between MLOps and DevOps lies in their focus and scope:

DevOps:

DevOps is a set of practices that combines software development (Dev) and IT operations (Ops) to improve the speed, quality, and reliability of software releases and deployments. DevOps focuses on the entire software development lifecycle, from coding to deployment, and aims to:

1. Automate testing, integration, and deployment processes
2. Improve collaboration between development and operations teams
3. Enhance monitoring, logging, and feedback mechanisms
4. Reduce time-to-market and increase release frequency

DevOps typically involves tools like Jenkins, Docker, Kubernetes, and Git, and is applied to a wide range of software applications, including web, mobile, and enterprise systems.

MLOps:

MLOps is a subset of DevOps that specifically focuses on the development, deployment, and maintenance of machine learning (ML) models and applications. MLOps aims to:

1. Streamline the ML model development process
2. Automate model testing, validation, and deployment
3. Ensure model reliability, scalability, and performance
4. Monitor model drift and retrain models as needed

MLOps involves tools like TensorFlow, PyTorch, Scikit-learn, and MLflow, and is applied to ML applications like predictive modeling, natural language processing, and computer vision.

Key differences:

1.   **Focus:** DevOps focuses on general software development, whileMLOps focuses on machine learning model development and deployment.
2.   **Scope:** DevOps encompasses the entire software developmentlifecycle, while MLOps is a subset of DevOps that specifically addresses ML model development and deployment.
3.   **Tools and techniques:** While there is some overlap, MLOps involvesspecialized tools and techniques, such as model serving, model monitoring, and data drift detection, which are not typically part of DevOps.
4.   **Challenges:** MLOps faces unique challenges, such as modelinterpretability, data quality, and concept drift, which are not as prominent in traditional DevOps.

In summary, DevOps is a broader discipline that encompasses software development and deployment, while MLOps is a specialized subset of DevOps that focuses on machine learning model development, deployment, and maintenance.

Q: What is the importance of version control for MLOps?

A: Version control is crucial for MLOps (Machine Learning Operations) as it enables teams to manage and track changes to their machine learning models, datasets, and codebases over time. The importance of version control for MLOps can be summarized as follows:

1.   **Reproducibility**: Version control allows teams to reproduce previousversions of their models, datasets, and code, which is essential for debugging, testing, and validation. By tracking changes, teams can identify what changes caused a particular issue or improvement.
2.   **Collaboration**: Version control enables multiple team members towork on the same project simultaneously without conflicts. Team members can make changes, commit them, and then merge them with the main branch, ensuring that everyone is working with the latest version.
3.   **Change management**: Version control helps teams manage changesto their models, datasets, and codebases. By tracking changes, teams can identify what changes were made, when they were made, and who made them, making it easier to manage and audit changes.
4.   **Model auditing and compliance**: Version control provides a clear audittrail of changes to models, datasets, and code, which is essential for regulatory compliance and model auditing. Teams can demonstrate that their models are transparent, explainable, and fair.

5. **Experiment tracking**: Version control allows teams to trackexperiments, including hyperparameter tuning, model selection, and dataset versions. This enables teams to compare the performance of different models and identify the best approach.

6. **Data versioning**: Version control helps teams manage differentversions of their datasets, including data preprocessing, feature engineering, and data augmentation. This ensures that teams are working with the correct version of the data.

7. **Model deployment**: Version control enables teams to track changes totheir models and deploy new versions of their models to production. This ensures that the correct version of the model is deployed and that changes are properly tested and validated.

8. **Rollback and recovery**: Version control allows teams to roll back toprevious versions of their models, datasets, and code in case of errors or issues. This ensures that teams can quickly recover from mistakes and minimize downtime.

To implement version control for MLOps, teams can use tools such as:

1. Git (e.g., GitHub, GitLab)
2. DVC (Data Version Control)
3. MLflow
4. TensorFlow Extended (TFX)
5. Kubeflow

By using version control, teams can ensure that their MLOps workflows are reproducible, collaborative, and auditable, which is essential for deploying reliable and high-performing machine learning models.

Q: Why is monitoring important in MLOps, and what metrics should you track?

A: Monitoring is a crucial aspect of MLOps (Machine Learning Operations) as it enables data scientists and engineers to track the performance of their machine learning models in production, identify potential issues, and make data-driven decisions to improve the models. Here are some reasons why monitoring is important in MLOps and what metrics you should track:

Why monitoring is important in MLOps:

1. **Model Drift Detection**: Monitoring helps detect model drift, whichoccurs when the data distribution changes over time, causing the model's performance to degrade.

2.   **Performance Optimization**: Monitoring enables you to identify areaswhere the model can be optimized, such as reducing latency or improving accuracy.

3.   **Error Detection**: Monitoring helps detect errors, such as data qualityissues, model failures, or incorrect predictions.

4.   **Compliance and Auditing**: Monitoring provides a record of modelperformance, which is essential for compliance and auditing purposes.

5.   **Continuous Improvement**: Monitoring allows you to refine andimprove the model over time, ensuring it remains accurate and effective.

Metrics to track in MLOps:

1. **Model Performance Metrics**:   *
Accuracy
* Precision
* Recall
* F1-score
* Mean Squared Error (MSE) * Mean Absolute Error (MAE) 2. **Data Quality Metrics**:
* Data distribution shifts
* Data missingness
* Data outliers
3. **Model Serving Metrics**:
* Request latency
* Response time
* Error rates
* Throughput
4. **Model Training Metrics**:
* Training time
* Training accuracy * Validation accuracy 5. **Business Metrics**:
* Revenue impact
* Customer satisfaction
* Return on Investment (ROI)
Additional considerations:

1.   **Monitoring frequency**: Monitor your models at regular intervals, suchas daily, weekly, or monthly, depending on the use case and data velocity.

2.   **Alerting and notification**: Set up alerting and notification systems tonotify teams when issues are detected, such as model drift or errors.

3.   **Visualization**: Use visualization tools to represent monitoring data,making it easier to understand and interpret.

4.   **Automated actions**: Implement automated actions, such as retrainingthe model or updating the serving infrastructure, in response to monitoring alerts.

By monitoring your machine learning models and tracking relevant metrics, you can ensure they continue to perform well, identify areas for improvement, and make data-driven decisions to drive business success.

Q: How would you implement a CI/CD pipeline for machine learning models?

A: Implementing a CI/CD Pipeline for Machine Learning Models

==

A Continuous Integration/Continuous Deployment (CI/CD) pipeline for machine learning models involves automating the testing, validation, and deployment of models to ensure they are reliable, efficient, and scalable. Here's a step-by-step guide to implementing a CI/CD pipeline for machine learning models:

Step 1: Define the Pipeline

*   Identify the machine learning model development workflow, including datapreparation, model training, testing, and deployment.
*   Determine the tools and technologies to be used in the pipeline, such asversion control systems (e.g., Git), containerization (e.g., Docker), and orchestration tools (e.g., Kubernetes).

Step 2: Set up Version Control and Collaboration

*   Use a version control system (e.g., Git) to track changes to the modelcode, data, and configuration files.
*   Set up a collaboration platform (e.g., GitHub, GitLab) to manage access,review code changes, and track issues.

Step 3: Automate Model Training and Testing

*   Write scripts to automate model training, testing, and validation using toolslike Apache Airflow, Apache Beam, or Python scripts.
*   Use libraries like scikit-learn, TensorFlow, or PyTorch to implementmachine learning algorithms.
*   Integrate testing frameworks like Pytest or Unittest to validate modelperformance.

Step 4: Implement Continuous Integration

*   Set up a CI tool (e.g., Jenkins, Travis CI, CircleCI) to automate the build,test, and validation process.
*   Configure the CI tool to run automated tests, validate model performance,and check for data quality issues.
*   Use containerization (e.g., Docker) to ensure consistent environments formodel training and testing.

Step 5: Implement Continuous Deployment

*   Set up a CD tool (e.g., Jenkins, Travis CI, CircleCI) to automate thedeployment process.
*   Configure the CD tool to deploy the model to a production environment(e.g., cloud, on-premises) after successful testing and validation.
*   Use orchestration tools (e.g., Kubernetes) to manage model deployment,scaling, and monitoring.

Step 6: Monitor and Log Model Performance

*   Set up monitoring tools (e.g., Prometheus, Grafana) to track modelperformance, latency, and other key metrics.
*   Use logging tools (e.g., ELK Stack) to collect and analyze model logs,errors, and exceptions.

Example Pipeline using Python and Docker

Here's an example pipeline using Python, Docker, and Jenkins:

```python
# model_training.py import
pandas as pd from
sklearn.ensemble import
RandomForestClassifier from
sklearn.model_selection
import train_test_split

# Load data
df = pd.read_csv('data.csv')
```

```python
# Split data into training and testing sets
X_train, X_test, y_train, y_test = train_test_split(df.drop('target', axis=1), df['target'],
test_size=0.2, random_state=42)

# Train model
model    =    RandomForestClassifier(n_estimators=100)    model.fit(X_train,
y_train)

# Save model import pickle with
open('model.pkl', 'wb') as f:
    pickle.dump(model, f)
```

```dockerfile    #
Dockerfile
FROM python:3.9-slim

# Set working directory
WORKDIR /app

# Copy requirements file COPY
requirements.txt .

# Install dependencies
RUN pip install -r requirements.txt

# Copy model training script COPY
model_training.py .

# Train model
RUN python model_training.py

# Save model
RUN mkdir -p /app/model
RUN cp model.pkl /app/model/
```

```groovy
// Jenkinsfile
pipeline {    agent
any
```

```
    stages {
stage('Build') {          steps
{
          sh 'docker build -t my-model .'
      }
    }
    stage('Test')               {
steps {
          sh 'docker run -t my-model python -m unittest discover -s tests'
      }
    }
    stage('Deploy') {
        steps {
          sh 'docker push my-model:latest'
          sh 'kubectl apply -f deployment.yaml'
        }
      }
    }
}
```

This example pipeline uses Python to train a machine learning model, Docker to containerize the model, and Jenkins to automate the build, test, and deployment process.

Best Practices
----

*   Use version control and collaboration platforms to manage modeldevelopment and deployment.
*   Automate model training, testing, and validation using scripts and CI/CDtools.
*   Use containerization and orchestration tools to ensure consistentenvironments and scalable deployment.
*   Monitor and log model performance to identify issues and improve modelreliability.
*   Implement continuous integration and deployment to ensure rapid andreliable model deployment.

Q: How do you implement model retraining in an automated MLOps pipeline

A: Implementing model retraining in an automated MLOps pipeline involves several steps:

1. **Monitoring**: Continuously monitor the performance of the deployedmodel using metrics such as accuracy, precision, recall, F1 score, and others. This can be done using tools like Prometheus, Grafana, or New Relic.
2. **Data Drift Detection**: Implement data drift detection to identifychanges in the data distribution, which can affect the model's performance. This can be done using techniques like statistical process control, Kolmogorov-Smirnov test, or machine learning-based methods.
3. **Retraining Trigger**: Set up a retraining trigger that initiates theretraining process when the model's performance drops below a certain threshold or when data drift is detected. This can be done using tools like Apache Airflow, Kubernetes, or AWS Step Functions.
4. **Data Preparation**: Prepare the new training data by collecting,preprocessing, and splitting it into training and validation sets. This can be done using tools like Apache Beam, Apache Spark, or scikit-learn.
5. **Model Retraining**: Retrain the model using the new training data andevaluate its performance on the validation set. This can be done using tools like TensorFlow, PyTorch, or scikit-learn.
6. **Model Evaluation**: Evaluate the performance of the retrained modelusing metrics such as accuracy, precision, recall, F1 score, and others.
7. **Model Deployment**: Deploy the retrained model to production,replacing the previous model. This can be done using tools like Docker, Kubernetes, or AWS SageMaker.
8. **Model Serving**: Serve the retrained model using a model servingplatform like TensorFlow Serving, AWS SageMaker, or Azure Machine Learning.

Automated MLOps Pipeline Tools:

1. **Apache Airflow**: A platform for programmatically defining, scheduling,and monitoring workflows.
2. **Kubernetes**: An container orchestration system for automatingdeployment, scaling, and management of containerized applications.
3. **AWS Step Functions**: A service for coordinating the components ofdistributed applications and microservices.
4. **Apache Beam**: A unified programming model for both batch andstreaming data processing.
5. **Apache Spark**: A unified analytics engine for large-scale dataprocessing.
6. **TensorFlow**: An open-source machine learning framework for buildingand training models.

7.   **PyTorch**: An open-source machine learning framework for buildingand training models.

8.   **scikit-learn**: An open-source machine learning library for building andtraining models.

Example Pipeline:

Here is an example pipeline using Apache Airflow and TensorFlow:

```python
from datetime import datetime, timedelta from
airflow import DAG
from airflow.operators.python_operator import PythonOperator
from airflow.operators.bash_operator import BashOperator from
tensorflow.keras.models import Sequential from
tensorflow.keras.layers import Dense

default_args = {
   'owner': 'airflow',
   'depends_on_past': False,
   'start_date': datetime(2023, 3, 21),
   'retries': 1,
   'retry_delay': timedelta(minutes=5),
}

dag = DAG(
   'model_retraining',    default_args=default_args,
   schedule_interval=timedelta(days=7),
)

def monitor_model_performance(**kwargs):
   # Monitor model performance using metrics like accuracy, precision, recall, F1 score
   # If performance drops below threshold, trigger retraining     if
performance < threshold:
      return 'retrain_model'
def retrain_model(**kwargs):
   # Prepare new training data
   # Retrain model using new training data    # Evaluate
model performance on validation set    model =
Sequential()
   model.add(Dense(64,            activation='relu',            input_shape=(784,)))
model.add(Dense(10, activation='softmax'))
```

```
    model.compile(optimizer='adam',                    loss='categorical_crossentropy',
metrics=['accuracy'])
              model.fit(X_train,    y_train,    epochs=10,    batch_size=128,
validation_data=(X_val, y_val))

def deploy_model(**kwargs):
   # Deploy retrained model to production    # Replace
previous model with retrained model
model.save('model.h5')

monitor_task = PythonOperator(
task_id='monitor_model_performance',
python_callable=monitor_model_performance,    dag=dag,
)

retrain_task = PythonOperator(
task_id='retrain_model',
python_callable=retrain_model,    dag=dag,
)

deploy_task = PythonOperator(
task_id='deploy_model',
python_callable=deploy_model,    dag=dag,
)

end_task = BashOperator(    task_id='end_task',
   bash_command='echo "Model retraining pipeline completed"',    dag=dag,
)

monitor_task >> retrain_task >> deploy_task >> end_task
```

This pipeline monitors the model's performance every 7 days, retrain the model if the performance drops below a certain threshold, and deploy the retrained model to production.

Q: What are the benefits and challenges of using serverless architectures for ML model deployment?

A: **Benefits of Serverless Architectures for ML Model Deployment:**

1.   **Scalability**: Serverless architectures can automatically scale to handlelarge volumes of requests, making them ideal for deploying machine learning (ML) models that require high throughput.

2.   **Cost-Effectiveness**: With serverless architectures, you only pay forthe compute resources used, reducing costs and minimizing waste.

3.   **Simplified Operations**: Serverless platforms handle infrastructuremanagement, patching, and maintenance, freeing up resources for ML model development and deployment.

4.   **Faster Deployment**: Serverless architectures enable rapid deployment of ML models, reducing the time and effort required to get models into production.

5.   **Improved Security**: Serverless platforms provide built-in securityfeatures, such as encryption and access controls, to protect ML models and data.

6.   **Flexibility**: Serverless architectures support a wide range ofprogramming languages and frameworks, making it easier to deploy ML models developed in different environments.

Challenges of Serverless Architectures for ML Model Deployment:

1.   **Cold Start**: Serverless functions can experience a "cold start" delaywhen invoked after a period of inactivity, which can impact performance and latency.

2.   **Limited Control**: With serverless architectures, you have limitedcontrol over the underlying infrastructure, which can make it difficult to optimize performance and debug issues.

3.   **Function Duration Limits**: Serverless platforms often have limits onthe duration of a function execution, which can be a challenge for ML models that require longer execution times.

4.   **Memory and Resource Constraints**: Serverless functions are subjectto memory and resource constraints, which can limit the complexity and size of ML models that can be deployed.

5.   **Debugging and Monitoring**: Debugging and monitoring serverlessfunctions can be more complex than traditional architectures, making it harder to identify and resolve issues.

6.   **Vendor Lock-In**: Serverless platforms can lead to vendor lock-in,making it difficult to move ML models to a different platform or environment.

7.   **Data Ingestion and Processing**: Serverless architectures can make itchallenging to handle large datasets and high-volume data ingestion, which can impact ML model performance and accuracy.

8.   **Model Drift and Updates**: Serverless architectures can make it difficultto update ML models in real-time, which can lead to model drift and decreased performance over time.

Best Practices for Deploying ML Models on Serverless Architectures:

1.   **Use containerization**: Containerize ML models to ensure consistencyand portability across different environments.
2.   **Optimize model size and complexity**: Optimize ML models to reducesize and complexity, making them more suitable for serverless deployment.
3.   **Use caching and memoization**: Implement caching and memoizationtechniques to reduce the impact of cold starts and improve performance.
4.   **Monitor and debug**: Implement monitoring and debugging tools toidentify and resolve issues quickly.
5.   **Choose the right serverless platform**: Select a serverless platform thatsupports your ML framework and language of choice, and provides the necessary resources and features for your use case.

Q: How do you ensure data security and compliance when deploying ML models in the cloud?

A: Ensuring data security and compliance when deploying machine learning (ML) models in the cloud is crucial to protect sensitive data and maintain regulatory requirements. Here are some measures to ensure data security and compliance:

Data Security Measures:

1.   **Data Encryption**: Encrypt data both in transit and at rest using secureprotocols such as SSL/TLS and AES.
2.   **Access Control**: Implement role-based access control (RBAC) andleast privilege access to ensure only authorized personnel can access and manage ML models and data.
3.   **Data Masking**: Mask sensitive data to prevent unauthorized accessand protect personally identifiable information (PII).
4.   **Data Storage**: Use secure cloud storage services such as AmazonS3, Google Cloud Storage, or Microsoft Azure Blob Storage, which provide robust security features.
5.   **Network Security**: Implement network security measures such asfirewalls, intrusion detection systems, and virtual private networks (VPNs) to protect against unauthorized access.

Compliance Measures:

1.   **Regulatory Compliance**: Familiarize yourself with relevant regulationssuch as GDPR, HIPAA, and CCPA, and ensure your ML model deployment meets these requirements.
2.   **Data Governance**: Establish a data governance framework to ensuredata quality, integrity, and security.
3.   **Model Explainability**: Implement model explainability techniques toensure transparency and accountability in ML model decision-making.
4.   **Audit Trails**: Maintain detailed audit trails to track all changes,updates, and access to ML models and data.
5.   **Compliance Certifications**: Obtain compliance certifications such asSOC 2, ISO 27001, or HITRUST to demonstrate adherence to industry standards.

Cloud Provider Security Features:

1.   **Cloud Provider Security**: Leverage cloud provider security featuressuch as Amazon Web Services (AWS) IAM, Google Cloud Identity and Access Management (IAM), or Microsoft Azure Active Directory (Azure AD).
2.   **Cloud Security Services**: Utilize cloud security services such as AWSCloudWatch, Google Cloud Security Command Center, or Microsoft Azure Security Center to monitor and respond to security threats.
3.   **Compliance Frameworks**: Use cloud provider compliance frameworkssuch as AWS Compliance Hub, Google Cloud Compliance, or Microsoft Azure Compliance to ensure regulatory compliance.

Best Practices:

1.   **Monitor and Update**: Regularly monitor and update ML models,dependencies, and libraries to ensure security and compliance.
2.   **Testing and Validation**: Perform thorough testing and validation of MLmodels to ensure accuracy, reliability, and security.
3.   **Documentation**: Maintain detailed documentation of ML modeldevelopment, deployment, and maintenance to ensure transparency and accountability.
4.   **Training and Awareness**: Provide training and awareness programsfor developers, data scientists, and other stakeholders on data security and compliance best practices.

By following these measures, you can ensure the security and compliance of your ML models when deploying them in the cloud.

Q: What strategies do you use for managing cloud costs associated with ML model training and deployment?

A: Managing cloud costs associated with ML model training and deployment is crucial to ensure cost-effectiveness and scalability. Here are some strategies that can be employed:

Model Training:

1.   **Right-Sizing Instances**: Choose the optimal instance type and size fortraining, taking into account factors like CPU, GPU, and memory requirements.
2.   **Spot Instances**: Utilize spot instances for non-time-sensitive trainingtasks, which can provide significant cost savings (up to 90%).
3.   **Reserved Instances**: Reserve instances for long-term, predictableworkloads, which can provide discounts (up to 75%).
4.   **Auto-Scaling**: Implement auto-scaling to dynamically adjust instancecounts based on workload demands.
5.   **Distributed Training**: Use distributed training techniques to splitworkloads across multiple instances, reducing the need for large, expensive instances.

Model Deployment:

1.   **Serverless Deployment**: Use serverless platforms (e.g., AWSLambda, Google Cloud Functions) for deploying models, which can reduce costs by only charging for actual usage.
2.   **Containerization**: Containerize models using Docker, Kubernetes, orother container orchestration tools to improve resource utilization and reduce costs.
3.   **Model Serving**: Use model serving platforms (e.g., TensorFlowServing, AWS SageMaker) to manage model deployment, scaling, and monitoring.
4.   **Edge Deployment**: Deploy models at the edge (e.g., on IoT devices,edge gateways) to reduce latency, bandwidth, and cloud costs.
5.   **Batch Processing**: Use batch processing for non-real-time inferenceworkloads, which can be more cost-effective than real-time processing.
Cost Monitoring and Optimization:

1.   **Cost Tracking**: Use cloud provider cost tracking tools (e.g., AWS CostExplorer, Google Cloud Cost Estimator) to monitor costs and identify areas for optimization.

2.   **Cost Allocation**: Allocate costs to specific projects, teams, ordepartments to improve cost transparency and accountability.

3.   **Cost Forecasting**: Use cost forecasting tools to predict future costsand identify opportunities for optimization.

4.   **Automated Cost Optimization**: Use automated cost optimization tools(e.g., ParkMyCloud, Turbonomic) to identify and implement cost-saving opportunities.

5.   **Regular Cost Audits**: Regularly perform cost audits to identify areasfor improvement and ensure cost-effectiveness.

Additional Strategies:

1.   **Data Storage Optimization**: Optimize data storage costs by usingefficient storage solutions (e.g., object storage, data lakes) and compressing data.

2.   **Data Transfer Optimization**: Minimize data transfer costs by usingdata transfer optimization techniques (e.g., data caching, data replication).

3.   **ML Framework Optimization**: Optimize ML frameworks (e.g.,TensorFlow, PyTorch) for performance and cost-effectiveness.

4.   **Model Pruning**: Prune models to reduce computational requirementsand costs.

5.   **Knowledge Sharing**: Share knowledge and best practices acrossteams to ensure consistent cost management and optimization.

By employing these strategies, organizations can effectively manage cloud costs associated with ML model training and deployment, ensuring cost-effectiveness, scalability, and reliability.

Q: How do you approach scaling ML models to handle increased user load?

A: Scaling Machine Learning (ML) models to handle increased user load involves a combination of data engineering, model optimization, and infrastructure scaling. Here's a step-by-step approach to help you scale your ML models:

Data Engineering

1.   **Data Ingestion**: Ensure that your data ingestion pipeline can handleincreased data volumes and velocities. Consider using distributed data processing frameworks like Apache Kafka, Apache Beam, or AWS Kinesis.

2.   **Data Storage**: Use scalable data storage solutions like distributeddatabases (e.g., Apache Cassandra, Google Bigtable), data lakes (e.g., Apache Hadoop, Amazon S3), or cloud-based storage services (e.g., Google Cloud Storage, Azure Blob Storage).

3.   **Data Preprocessing**: Implement efficient data preprocessingtechniques, such as data parallelism, to reduce the computational overhead of data preparation.

Model Optimization

1.   **Model Pruning**: Remove unnecessary model parameters to reducecomputational complexity and improve inference speed.
2.   **Knowledge Distillation**: Train smaller models to mimic the behavior oflarger models, reducing computational requirements.
3.   **Quantization**: Represent model weights and activations usinglower-precision data types (e.g., int8 instead of float32) to reduce memory usage and improve inference speed.
4.   **Model Serving**: Use model serving platforms like TensorFlow Serving,AWS SageMaker, or Azure Machine Learning to manage model deployment, updates, and scaling.

Infrastructure Scaling

1.   **Horizontal Scaling**: Add more machines to your cluster to increaseprocessing capacity. Use containerization (e.g., Docker) and orchestration tools (e.g., Kubernetes) to manage and scale your infrastructure.
2.   **Vertical Scaling**: Increase the computational resources (e.g., CPU,GPU, memory) of individual machines to improve processing capacity.
3.   **Cloud Services**: Leverage cloud services like AWS SageMaker,Google Cloud AI Platform, or Azure Machine Learning to scale your ML infrastructure and take advantage of managed services.
4.   **Load Balancing**: Distribute incoming traffic across multiple instancesto ensure efficient resource utilization and minimize downtime.
5.   **Auto-Scaling**: Implement auto-scaling mechanisms to dynamicallyadjust the number of instances based on changing workload demands.

Monitoring and Optimization

1.   **Model Performance Monitoring**: Track model performance metrics(e.g., accuracy, latency, throughput) to identify bottlenecks and areas for optimization.
2.   **Resource Utilization Monitoring**: Monitor resource utilization (e.g.,CPU, memory, disk usage) to identify potential bottlenecks and optimize resource allocation.
3.   **Continuous Integration and Deployment (CI/CD)**: Implement CI/CDpipelines to automate model training, testing, and deployment, ensuring that changes are properly validated and rolled out.

By following these steps, you can effectively scale your ML models to handle increased user load and ensure a seamless user experience.

Example Use Case:

Suppose you're building a recommendation system for an e-commerce platform. To scale your ML model, you:

1.   Implement a distributed data processing pipeline using Apache Kafkaand Apache Spark to handle increased data volumes.
2.   Optimize your model using model pruning, knowledge distillation, andquantization to reduce computational complexity.
3.   Deploy your model using TensorFlow Serving and scale yourinfrastructure using Kubernetes and Google Cloud AI Platform.
4.   Monitor model performance and resource utilization using Prometheusand Grafana, and implement auto-scaling to adjust instance counts based on changing workload demands.

By following this approach, you can ensure that your recommendation system can handle increased user load and provide a seamless user experience.

Q: Explain the typical lifecycle of an MLOps pipeline.

A: The typical lifecycle of an MLOps (Machine Learning Operations) pipeline involves several stages that enable the efficient development, deployment, and maintenance of machine learning (ML) models. Here's an overview of the MLOps pipeline lifecycle:

1.   **Data Ingestion**: This stage involves collecting and processing datafrom various sources, such as databases, APIs, or files. The data is then stored in a centralized location, like a data lake or data warehouse, for further processing.
2.   **Data Preparation**: In this stage, the collected data is cleaned,transformed, and formatted to prepare it for model training. This includes handling missing values, data normalization, and feature engineering.
3.   **Model Development**: Data scientists develop and train ML modelsusing the prepared data. This stage involves selecting the most suitable algorithm, hyperparameter tuning, and model evaluation.
4.   **Model Training**: The ML model is trained on the prepared data, andthe model's performance is evaluated using metrics such as accuracy, precision, and recall.
5.   **Model Evaluation**: The trained model is evaluated on a test dataset toassess its performance and identify potential biases or areas for improvement.

6.   **Model Deployment**: The trained and evaluated model is deployed to aproduction environment, where it can receive input data and generate predictions or outputs.

7.   **Model Serving**: The deployed model is served to users orapplications, which can interact with the model through APIs or other interfaces.

8.   **Model Monitoring**: The deployed model is continuously monitored forperformance, data drift, and concept drift. This stage involves tracking metrics such as accuracy, latency, and throughput.

9.   **Model Maintenance**: Based on the monitoring results, the model isupdated, retrained, or re-deployed as needed to maintain its performance and adapt to changing data distributions or business requirements.

10.   **Model Retraining**: The model is retrained on new data or updateddata to maintain its performance and adapt to changing data distributions or business requirements.

11.   **Model Versioning**: Different versions of the model are tracked andmanaged to ensure reproducibility, auditing, and rollbacks.

Throughout the MLOps pipeline lifecycle, automation, and continuous integration/continuous deployment (CI/CD) practices are applied to ensure efficient, reliable, and scalable model development, deployment, and maintenance.

Key MLOps pipeline components:

* **Data pipeline**: manages data ingestion, preparation, and storage* **Model pipeline**: manages model development, training, evaluation, and deployment
* **Serving pipeline**: manages model serving and monitoring
* **Monitoring and logging**: tracks model performance, data quality, andsystem health
* **Automation and CI/CD**: automates pipeline workflows, testing, anddeployment

By following the MLOps pipeline lifecycle, organizations can streamline their ML development and deployment processes, reduce errors, and improve model performance, ultimately leading to faster time-to-market and increased business value.

Q: How do you handle data quality issues in an MLOps pipeline?

A: Handling data quality issues in an MLOps pipeline is crucial to ensure that machine learning models are trained and deployed with accurate and reliable data. Here are some steps to handle data quality issues in an MLOps pipeline:

1.   **Data Ingestion**: Implement data validation and cleansing at the dataingestion stage to detect and correct errors early on. This includes checking for missing values, outliers, and data type inconsistencies.

2.   **Data Profiling**: Perform data profiling to understand the distribution ofdata, identify patterns, and detect anomalies. This helps to identify potential data quality issues and inform data preprocessing steps.

3.   **Data Preprocessing**: Implement data preprocessing steps to handlemissing values, outliers, and data normalization. This includes techniques such as imputation, transformation, and feature scaling.

4.   **Data Validation**: Validate data against a set of predefined rules andconstraints to ensure data accuracy and consistency. This includes checks for data type, format, and range.

5.   **Data Quality Monitoring**: Continuously monitor data quality metrics,such as data completeness, accuracy, and consistency, to detect issues and anomalies in real-time.

6.   **Data Lineage**: Maintain data lineage to track the origin, processing,and transformation of data. This helps to identify the source of data quality issues and inform data correction and improvement efforts.

7.   **Automated Testing**: Implement automated testing to validate dataquality and detect issues early on. This includes unit testing, integration testing, and regression testing.

8.   **Human-in-the-Loop**: Involve human reviewers and domain experts tovalidate data quality and provide feedback on data accuracy and relevance.

9.   **Data Correction**: Implement data correction mechanisms to addressdata quality issues, such as data imputation, data transformation, and data deletion.

10.   **Continuous Improvement**: Continuously review and refine dataquality processes to ensure that data quality issues are addressed and prevented in the future.

Tools and Techniques:

1.   **Data Quality Frameworks**: Utilize data quality frameworks, such asApache Beam, Apache Spark, and Great Expectations, to implement data quality checks and validation.

2.   **Data Profiling Tools**: Use data profiling tools, such as pandas,NumPy, and Matplotlib, to understand data distribution and identify patterns.

3.   **Data Preprocessing Libraries**: Utilize data preprocessing libraries,such as scikit-learn and TensorFlow, to implement data preprocessing steps.

4.   **Data Validation Libraries**: Use data validation libraries, such asPydantic and Cerberus, to validate data against predefined rules and constraints.

5.   **Monitoring and Alerting Tools**: Implement monitoring and alertingtools, such as Prometheus, Grafana, and PagerDuty, to detect data quality issues and notify stakeholders.

Best Practices:

1.   **Define Data Quality Metrics**: Define clear data quality metrics andthresholds to measure data quality.
2.   **Implement Data Quality Checks**: Implement data quality checks andvalidation at every stage of the MLOps pipeline.
3.   **Use Automated Testing**: Use automated testing to validate dataquality and detect issues early on.
4.   **Involve Human Reviewers**: Involve human reviewers and domainexperts to validate data quality and provide feedback.
5.   **Continuously Review and Refine**: Continuously review and refine dataquality processes to ensure that data quality issues are addressed and prevented in the future.

Deep Learning

Q: What is feed forward network and how it is different from recurrent neural network?

A: **Feed Forward Network (FFN) vs Recurrent Neural Network (RNN)**

Overview

Both Feed Forward Networks (FFNs) and Recurrent Neural Networks (RNNs) are types of artificial neural networks used in deep learning. The primary difference between them lies in the way they process input data and the connections between their nodes.

Feed Forward Network (FFN)

A Feed Forward Network is a type of neural network where the data flows only in one direction, from input layer to output layer, without any feedback loops. Each layer consists of multiple nodes (neurons) that receive input from the previous layer, perform a computation, and then send the output to the next layer.

Key characteristics of FFNs:

* Data flows only in one direction (input -> hidden layers -> output)
* No feedback loops or recurrent connections

* Each layer processes the input independently
* Well-suited for tasks with fixed-size input and output, such as imageclassification, regression, and classification

Recurrent Neural Network (RNN)

A Recurrent Neural Network is a type of neural network where the data flows in a sequence, and the output from the previous time step is used as input for the next time step. This creates a feedback loop, allowing the network to keep track of information over time.

Key characteristics of RNNs:

*   Data flows in a sequence, with feedback loops (input -> hidden state ->output -> next input)
*   Recurrent connections allow the network to maintain a hidden state overtime
*   Each time step processes the input and the previous hidden state* Well-suited for tasks with sequential data, such as language modeling, speech recognition, and time series forecasting

Key differences

1.   **Direction of data flow**: FFNs have a one-way flow of data, while RNNshave a feedback loop that allows data to flow in a sequence.
2.   **Recurrent connections**: RNNs have recurrent connections that allowthe network to maintain a hidden state over time, while FFNs do not.
3.   **Input and output structure**: FFNs typically have fixed-size input andoutput, while RNNs can handle sequential data with varying lengths.
4.   **Applications**: FFNs are commonly used for tasks like imageclassification, regression, and classification, while RNNs are used for tasks like language modeling, speech recognition, and time series forecasting.

In summary, Feed Forward Networks are suitable for tasks with fixed-size input and output, while Recurrent Neural Networks are better suited for tasks with sequential data and varying lengths.

Q: What is the forward and backward propogations in deep learning?

A: **Forward Propagation and Backward Propagation in Deep Learning**

In deep learning, forward propagation and backward propagation are two essential processes used in training artificial neural networks.

Forward Propagation

Forward propagation, also known as the **forward pass**, is the process of passing input data through a neural network to obtain the output. The steps involved in forward propagation are:

1. **Input**: The input data is fed into the network.
2. **Linear Transformation**: The input data is transformed using lineartransformations, such as matrix multiplication and addition.
3. **Activation Function**: The output of the linear transformation is passedthrough an activation function, which introduces non-linearity into the model.
4. **Output**: The output of the activation function is passed to the nextlayer, and this process is repeated until the final output is obtained.

The forward propagation process can be represented mathematically as:

`output = ?(W * input + b)`

where `?` is the activation function, `W` is the weight matrix, `input` is the input data, and `b` is the bias term.

Backward Propagation

Backward propagation, also known as the **backward pass**, is the process of calculating the error between the predicted output and the actual output, and then adjusting the model's parameters to minimize this error. The steps involved in backward propagation are:

1.   **Error Calculation**: The error between the predicted output and theactual output is calculated using a loss function, such as mean squared error or cross-entropy.
2.   **Gradient Calculation**: The gradient of the loss function with respect toeach of the model's parameters is calculated using the chain rule.
3.   **Parameter Update**: The model's parameters are updated using anoptimization algorithm, such as stochastic gradient descent (SGD), to minimize the loss function.

The backward propagation process can be represented mathematically as:

`?W = -? * (dE/dW)`

where `?W` is the change in the weight matrix, `?` is the learning rate, and `dE/dW` is the gradient of the loss function with respect to the weight matrix.

Example Code

Here is an example code in Python using the PyTorch library to demonstrate forward and backward propagation:

```python
import torch import
torch.nn as nn import
torch.optim as optim

# Define a simple neural network
class Net(nn.Module):    def
__init__(self):

        super(Net, self).__init__()
        self.fc1 = nn.Linear(784, 128)  # input layer (28x28 images) -> hidden layer (128
units)
        self.fc2 = nn.Linear(128, 10)  # hidden layer (128 units) -> output layer
(10 units)

    def forward(self, x):
        x = torch.relu(self.fc1(x))  # activation function for hidden layer       x
= self.fc2(x)       return x

# Initialize the network, loss function, and optimizer net =
Net()
criterion = nn.CrossEntropyLoss()
optimizer = optim.SGD(net.parameters(), lr=0.01)

# Forward propagation
input_data = torch.randn(1, 784)  # random input data output =
net(input_data)

# Backward propagation
target = torch.tensor([0])  # actual output loss =
criterion(output, target)
loss.backward()
optimizer.step()
```

```
```
```

In this example, the `forward` method defines the forward propagation process, and the `backward` method is used to calculate the gradients of the loss function with respect to the model's parameters. The `optimizer` is used to update the model's parameters to minimize the loss function.

**Q: What is backpropagation, and how does it work in training neural networks?**

A: **Introduction to Backpropagation**
=====================================

Backpropagation is a widely used algorithm in training neural networks, particularly in the field of deep learning. It is an essential component of the training process, allowing the network to learn from its mistakes and improve its performance over time.

**What is Backpropagation?**
---------------------------

Backpropagation is a method for training neural networks by minimizing the error between the network's predictions and the actual outputs. The algorithm works by propagating the error backwards through the network, adjusting the weights and biases of the neurons to minimize the loss function.

**How Backpropagation Works**
----------------------------

The backpropagation algorithm involves the following steps:

1.      **Forward Pass**: The network processes the input data and producesan output.
2.      **Error Calculation**: The difference between the predicted output andthe actual output is calculated, resulting in an error value.
3.      **Backward Pass**: The error is propagated backwards through thenetwork, adjusting the weights and biases of the neurons to minimize the loss function.
4.      **Weight Update**: The weights and biases of the neurons are updatedbased on the calculated error and the learning rate.

**Mathematical Formulation**
---------------------------

The backpropagation algorithm can be formulated mathematically as follows:
```

*   **Loss Function**: The loss function is defined as the difference betweenthe predicted output and the actual output, typically measured using mean squared error (MSE) or cross-entropy loss.

*   **Gradient Descent**: The gradient descent algorithm is used to minimizethe loss function, adjusting the weights and biases of the neurons to minimize the error.

*   **Chain Rule**: The chain rule is used to compute the gradients of theloss function with respect to the weights and biases of the neurons.

Example Code

Here is an example code snippet in Python using the Keras library to demonstrate the backpropagation algorithm:

```python
# Import necessary libraries from
keras.models import Sequential from
keras.layers import Dense from
keras.optimizers import SGD from
keras.utils import to_categorical from
sklearn.datasets import load_iris
from sklearn.model_selection import train_test_split

# Load iris dataset iris
= load_iris() X =
iris.data y = iris.target

# Split dataset into training and testing sets
X_train,  X_test,  y_train,  y_test  =  train_test_split(X,  y,  test_size=0.2,
random_state=42)

# One-hot encode labels y_train =
to_categorical(y_train) y_test =
to_categorical(y_test)

# Define neural network model model =
Sequential()
model.add(Dense(64,  activation='relu',  input_shape=(4,)))  model.add(Dense(3,
activation='softmax'))

# Compile model
```

```
model.compile(loss='categorical_crossentropy', optimizer=SGD(lr=0.01),
metrics=['accuracy'])

# Train model
model.fit(X_train,      y_train,       epochs=10,     batch_size=32,
validation_data=(X_test, y_test))
```

In this example, the backpropagation algorithm is used to train a neural network to classify iris flowers into three species. The `SGD` optimizer is used to update the weights and biases of the neurons, and the `categorical_crossentropy` loss function is used to measure the error between the predicted output and the actual output.

Conclusion

Backpropagation is a fundamental algorithm in training neural networks, allowing the network to learn from its mistakes and improve its performance over time. By propagating the error backwards through the network and adjusting the weights and biases of the neurons, the backpropagation algorithm enables the network to minimize the loss function and achieve optimal performance.

Q: What is the vanishing gradient and exploding gradient problem, and how can it affect neural network training?

A: The vanishing gradient and exploding gradient problems are two common issues that can affect the training of neural networks, particularly those with multiple layers. These problems arise during the backpropagation process, where the gradients of the loss function are computed and used to update the model's weights.

Vanishing Gradient Problem:

The vanishing gradient problem occurs when the gradients of the loss function become very small as they are backpropagated through the network. This can happen when the activation functions used in the network, such as sigmoid or tanh, have a small derivative. As a result, the gradients are multiplied together, causing them to become smaller and smaller, until they become negligible.

When the gradients are very small, the weights of the network are not updated significantly, making it difficult for the network to learn. This can lead to:

* Slow convergence or non-convergence of the training process
* Weights that are not updated correctly, resulting in poor modelperformance

* Difficulty in training deep networks, as the gradients become smaller witheach additional layer

Exploding Gradient Problem:

The exploding gradient problem is the opposite of the vanishing gradient problem. It occurs when the gradients of the loss function become very large as they are backpropagated through the network. This can happen when the activation functions used in the network, such as ReLU, have a large derivative.
When the gradients are very large, the weights of the network are updated too aggressively, causing the model to overshoot the optimal solution. This can lead to:

* Oscillations in the training process, making it difficult to converge
* Weights that are updated too quickly, resulting in poor model performance* Difficulty in training deep networks, as the gradients become larger with each additional layer

Causes of Vanishing and Exploding Gradients:

The vanishing and exploding gradient problems can be caused by several factors, including:

* **Activation functions:** The choice of activation function can affect themagnitude of the gradients. Sigmoid and tanh functions can cause vanishing gradients, while ReLU can cause exploding gradients.
* **Network depth:** Deeper networks are more prone to vanishing andexploding gradients, as the gradients are multiplied together more times. * **Weight initialization:** Poor weight initialization can lead to large or small gradients, exacerbating the vanishing or exploding gradient problem. * **Learning rate:** A high learning rate can cause exploding gradients, while a low learning rate can cause vanishing gradients.

Solutions to Vanishing and Exploding Gradients:

Several techniques can be used to mitigate the vanishing and exploding gradient problems:

* **ReLU and its variants:** Using ReLU or its variants, such as LeakyReLU or Parametric ReLU, can help alleviate the vanishing gradient problem.
* **Batch normalization:** Normalizing the inputs to each layer can helpreduce the effect of vanishing and exploding gradients.

* **Gradient clipping:** Clipping the gradients to a maximum value canprevent exploding gradients.
* **Weight regularization:** Regularizing the weights can help prevent largeweights and reduce the effect of exploding gradients.
* **Learning rate schedulers:** Using a learning rate scheduler can helpadjust the learning rate during training to prevent vanishing or exploding gradients.
* **Residual connections:** Using residual connections can help alleviatethe vanishing gradient problem by providing a path for the gradients to flow through.

By understanding the causes of vanishing and exploding gradients and using these techniques, you can improve the stability and performance of your neural network models.

Q: How do you prevent overfitting in neural networks?

A: Preventing overfitting in neural networks is crucial to ensure that the model generalizes well to new, unseen data. Overfitting occurs when a model is too complex and learns the noise in the training data, resulting in poor performance on test data. Here are some techniques to prevent overfitting in neural networks:

1.   **Regularization**: Regularization techniques, such as L1 and L2 regularization, add a penalty term to the loss function to discourage large weights. This helps to prevent the model from overfitting to the training data.
2.   **Dropout**: Dropout is a technique where a fraction of the neurons arerandomly dropped during training. This helps to prevent the model from relying too heavily on any individual neuron, reducing overfitting.
3.   **Early Stopping**: Early stopping involves stopping the training processwhen the model's performance on the validation set starts to degrade. This helps to prevent the model from overfitting to the training data.
4.   **Data Augmentation**: Data augmentation involves generatingadditional training data by applying transformations to the existing data, such as rotation, scaling, and flipping. This helps to increase the size of the training dataset and prevent overfitting.
5.   **Batch Normalization**: Batch normalization involves normalizing theinput data for each layer, which helps to reduce the effect of internal covariate shift and prevent overfitting.
6.   **Reducing Model Complexity**: Reducing the number of layers,neurons, or parameters in the model can help to prevent overfitting. This can be done by using a smaller model or by pruning the model.
7.   **Using a Larger Dataset**: Using a larger dataset can help to preventoverfitting, as the model is less likely to overfit to the noise in the data.

8.   **Ensemble Methods**: Ensemble methods, such as bagging andboosting, involve combining the predictions of multiple models to reduce overfitting.

9.   **Weight Decay**: Weight decay involves adding a penalty term to theloss function to discourage large weights.

10.   **Gradient Clipping**: Gradient clipping involves clipping the gradientsto prevent them from exploding, which can help to prevent overfitting.

By using these techniques, you can help to prevent overfitting in neural networks and improve the model's performance on new, unseen data.

Example Code (Python):
```python
from keras.layers import Dropout, BatchNormalization from keras.regularizers import l2

# Define a neural network model with dropout and L2 regularization model = Sequential()
model.add(Dense(64,           activation='relu',           input_shape=(784,)))
model.add(Dropout(0.2))
model.add(Dense(32, activation='relu', kernel_regularizer=l2(0.01)))
model.add(BatchNormalization()) model.add(Dense(10,
activation='softmax'))

# Compile the model
model.compile(optimizer='adam',      loss='categorical_crossentropy',
metrics=['accuracy'])
```

In this example, we define a neural network model with dropout and L2 regularization to prevent overfitting. The `Dropout` layer is used to randomly drop 20% of the neurons during training, and the `l2` regularizer is used to add a penalty term to the loss function to discourage large weights. The `BatchNormalization` layer is used to normalize the input data for each layer.

Q: What is dropout, and how does it help in training neural networks?

A: **Dropout: A Regularization Technique**
=======================================

Dropout is a regularization technique used in training neural networks to prevent overfitting. It was introduced by Geoffrey Hinton and his colleagues in 2012.

What is Dropout?

Dropout is a technique where a fraction of the neurons in a neural network are randomly dropped out during training. This means that the output of these neurons is set to zero, and the weights connected to these neurons are not updated during backpropagation.

How Does Dropout Help?

Dropout helps in training neural networks in several ways:

1.   **Prevents Overfitting**: By randomly dropping out neurons, dropoutprevents the network from relying too heavily on any single neuron or group of neurons. This helps to prevent overfitting, which occurs when a network becomes too specialized to the training data and fails to generalize well to new data.
2.   **Encourages Ensemble Learning**: Dropout can be seen as a way oftraining an ensemble of neural networks. Each time a neuron is dropped out, the network is forced to learn a different representation of the data. This encourages the network to learn multiple representations, which can lead to better generalization performance.
3.   **Reduces Co-Adaptation**: Dropout helps to reduce co-adaptationbetween neurons. Co-adaptation occurs when neurons learn to rely on each other to make predictions, rather than learning to make predictions independently. By dropping out neurons, dropout encourages each neuron to learn to make predictions independently, which can lead to better generalization performance.

How to Implement Dropout

Dropout is typically implemented by adding a dropout layer to a neural network. This layer randomly sets the output of a fraction of the neurons to zero during training. The fraction of neurons to drop out is a hyperparameter that needs to be tuned.

Example Code (PyTorch)
```python import torch import
torch.nn as nn import
torch.nn.functional as F
```

```
class Net(nn.Module):     def
__init__(self):
    super(Net, self).__init__()
    self.fc1 = nn.Linear(784, 128)  # input layer (28x28 images) -> hidden layer (128
units)
    self.dropout = nn.Dropout(p=0.2)  # dropout layer with p=0.2
    self.fc2 = nn.Linear(128, 10)  # hidden layer (128 units) -> output layer
(10 units)

  def forward(self, x):
    x = F.relu(self.fc1(x))  # activation function for hidden layer       x =
self.dropout(x)  # dropout layer
    x = self.fc2(x)       return
x

# Initialize the network and optimizer net =
Net()
optimizer = torch.optim.SGD(net.parameters(), lr=0.01)

# Train the network for epoch in range(10):    for x, y
in train_loader:      x = x.view(-1, 784)  # flatten the
input data      optimizer.zero_grad()       output =
net(x)
    loss = F.cross_entropy(output, y)
loss.backward()      optimizer.step() ```
```

In this example, the `nn.Dropout` layer is used to drop out 20% of the neurons in the hidden layer during training. The `p` parameter of the `nn.Dropout` layer specifies the fraction of neurons to drop out.

Q: How do you choose the number of layers and neurons for a neural network?

A: Choosing the number of layers and neurons for a neural network is a complex task, and there's no one-size-fits-all solution. However, here are some general guidelines to help you make an informed decision:

Number of Layers:

1.   **Simple problems:** For simple problems, such as linear regression orbinary classification, a single layer with a small number of neurons (e.g., 2-10) might be sufficient.

2.   **Moderate complexity:** For problems with moderate complexity, suchas multi-class classification or regression with non-linear relationships, 2-3 layers with 10-100 neurons per layer might be a good starting point.

3.   **Complex problems:** For complex problems, such as image or speechrecognition, 4-10 layers with 100-1000 neurons per layer might be necessary.

Number of Neurons per Layer:

1.   **Input layer:** The number of neurons in the input layer is determined bythe number of features in your dataset.

2.   **Hidden layers:** The number of neurons in hidden layers can bedetermined using the following rules of thumb:

* For small datasets (<1000 samples), use fewer neurons (e.g., 2-10).

* For medium-sized datasets (1000-10000 samples), use a moderatenumber of neurons (e.g., 10-50).

* For large datasets (>10000 samples), use more neurons (e.g., 50-100).

3. **Output layer:** The number of neurons in the output layer is determined by the number of classes or outputs in your problem.

Other Considerations:

1.   **Overfitting:** Using too many layers or neurons can lead to overfitting,especially when dealing with small datasets. Regularization techniques, such as dropout or L1/L2 regularization, can help mitigate this issue.

2.   **Computational resources:** Increasing the number of layers andneurons can significantly increase computational requirements. Consider the available computational resources and the training time when designing your network.

3.   **Activation functions:** The choice of activation functions can alsoimpact the number of layers and neurons required. For example, using ReLU (Rectified Linear Unit) activation functions can reduce the number of neurons needed compared to using sigmoid or tanh activation functions.

Hyperparameter Tuning:

1.   **Grid search:** Perform a grid search over a range of possible layer andneuron configurations to find the optimal combination.

2.   **Random search:** Use random search to sample a subset of possibleconfigurations and evaluate their performance.

3.   **Bayesian optimization:** Use Bayesian optimization techniques, suchas Gaussian process optimization or tree-based optimization, to search for the optimal configuration.

Example Code (Python with Keras):

```python
from keras.models import Sequential
from keras.layers import Dense from
keras.optimizers import Adam
from sklearn.model_selection import train_test_split
from sklearn.datasets import load_iris from
sklearn.metrics import accuracy_score

# Load iris dataset iris
= load_iris() X =
iris.data y = iris.target

# Split dataset into training and testing sets
X_train,   X_test,   y_train,   y_test   =   train_test_split(X,   y,   test_size=0.2,
random_state=42)

# Define neural network architecture model =
Sequential()
model.add(Dense(10, activation='relu', input_shape=(4,)))
model.add(Dense(10, activation='relu')) model.add(Dense(3,
activation='softmax'))

# Compile model
model.compile(loss='sparse_categorical_crossentropy',   optimizer=Adam(lr=0.001),
metrics=['accuracy'])

# Train model
model.fit(X_train,            y_train,            epochs=10,            batch_size=32,
validation_data=(X_test, y_test))

# Evaluate model
y_pred  =  model.predict(X_test)  y_pred_class  =
y_pred.argmax(axis=1)
print('Accuracy:', accuracy_score(y_test, y_pred_class))
```

In this example, we define a neural network with 2 hidden layers, each with 10
neurons, and an output layer with 3 neurons. We then train the model using the Adam

optimizer and evaluate its performance on the test set. You can modify the architecture and hyperparameters to suit your specific problem.

Q: What is transfer learning, and how is it applied in deep learning?

A: Transfer learning is a machine learning technique where a model trained on one task is re-purposed or fine-tuned for another related task. In deep learning, transfer learning is particularly useful because it allows us to leverage pre-trained models and their learned features to improve performance on a new, but related task.

Why Transfer Learning?

1.   **Reduced training time**: Training a deep neural network from scratchcan be computationally expensive and time-consuming. Transfer learning allows us to start with a pre-trained model and fine-tune it for our specific task, reducing the training time.
2.   **Improved performance**: Pre-trained models have already learned torecognize general features and patterns in data, which can be useful for our specific task. By fine-tuning these models, we can adapt them to our task and improve performance.
3.   **Small dataset**: When we have a small dataset for our specific task,transfer learning can help by providing a pre-trained model that has already learned to recognize patterns in a larger dataset.

How Transfer Learning is Applied in Deep Learning

1.   **Pre-trained models**: Many pre-trained models are available, such asVGG16, ResNet50, and BERT, which have been trained on large datasets like ImageNet, CIFAR-10, and Wikipedia.
2.   **Freezing and fine-tuning**: We can freeze the weights of thepre-trained model and add a new layer on top, which is then fine-tuned for our specific task. Alternatively, we can fine-tune the entire pre-trained model, but this requires more computational resources.
3.   **Domain adaptation**: Transfer learning can be used for domainadaptation, where a model trained on one domain (e.g., images of dogs) is adapted for another domain (e.g., images of cats).
4.   **Multi-task learning**: Transfer learning can be used for multi-tasklearning, where a single model is trained on multiple tasks simultaneously.

Examples of Transfer Learning in Deep Learning

1.   **Image classification**: Using a pre-trained VGG16 model for imageclassification tasks, such as classifying images of animals.
2.   **Natural Language Processing (NLP)**: Using a pre-trained BERTmodel for NLP tasks, such as sentiment analysis or question answering.
3.   **Object detection**: Using a pre-trained YOLO (You Only Look Once) model for object detection tasks, such as detecting pedestrians or cars.

Best Practices for Transfer Learning

1.   **Choose a suitable pre-trained model**: Select a pre-trained model thatis relevant to your task and has been trained on a similar dataset.
2.   **Fine-tune the model**: Fine-tune the pre-trained model on your specifictask to adapt it to your dataset.
3.   **Monitor performance**: Monitor the performance of the model on yourvalidation set to avoid overfitting.
4.   **Regularization techniques**: Use regularization techniques, such asdropout and L1/L2 regularization, to prevent overfitting.

In summary, transfer learning is a powerful technique in deep learning that allows us to leverage pre-trained models and their learned features to improve performance on a new, but related task. By applying transfer learning, we can reduce training time, improve performance, and achieve state-of-the-art results on a wide range of tasks.

Generative AI

Q: Write a function that uses the GPT-2 model to generate a short story based on a user-provided prompt

A: **GPT-2 Short Story Generator**

==

This code uses the Hugging Face Transformers library to load the GPT-2 model and generate a short story based on a user-provided prompt.

Requirements
----

* Python 3.8+
* Hugging Face Transformers library (`transformers`)* PyTorch library (`torch`)

Code

```python
import torch
from transformers import GPT2Tokenizer, GPT2LMHeadModel

def generate_short_story(prompt, max_length=100, temperature=0.7):
    """
    Generate a short story based on a user-provided prompt using the GPT-2 model.

    Args:
        prompt (str): The user-provided prompt.
        max_length (int, optional): The maximum length of the generated story. Defaults to 100.
        temperature (float, optional): The temperature parameter for the GPT-2 model. Defaults to 0.7.

    Returns:
        str: The generated short story.
    """
    # Load the GPT-2 model and tokenizer
    model = GPT2LMHeadModel.from_pretrained('gpt2')    tokenizer = GPT2Tokenizer.from_pretrained('gpt2')
    # Encode the prompt
```

```
input_ids = tokenizer.encode(prompt, return_tensors='pt')

    # Generate the short story
    output = model.generate(      input_ids,
        max_length=max_length,
temperature=temperature,
do_sample=True,       top_k=50,
        top_p=0.95
    )

    # Decode the generated story
    story = tokenizer.decode(output[0], skip_special_tokens=True)    return story

# Example usage
prompt = "In a world where magic was real, a young girl named Lily discovered she had the power to" story = generate_short_story(prompt) print(story) ```
```

Explanation

----

1. The `generate_short_story` function takes a prompt, maximum length,and temperature as input.
2. It loads the GPT-2 model and tokenizer using the Hugging FaceTransformers library.
3. The prompt is encoded into input IDs using the tokenizer.
4. The `generate` method of the GPT-2 model is used to generate the shortstory. The `max_length` parameter controls the length of the generated story, and the `temperature` parameter controls the level of randomness in the generation process.
5. The generated story is decoded from the output IDs using the tokenizer.
6. The decoded story is returned as a string.

Tips and Variations

----

* Experiment with different temperature values to control the level ofcreativity in the generated story.
* Use a longer prompt to provide more context for the story.
* Try using different GPT-2 models, such as `gpt2-medium` or `gpt2-large`,for more complex and detailed stories.
* Use the `top_k` and `top_p` parameters to control the diversity of thegenerated story.

* Consider using a more advanced decoding strategy, such as beam searchor sampling, for more coherent and engaging stories.

Q: Explain the difference between generative and discriminative models?

A: Generative and discriminative models are two fundamental types of machine learning models that serve distinct purposes.

Discriminative Models:
Discriminative models, also known as conditional models, are designed to predict the probability of a specific class or label given a set of input features. Their primary goal is to learn a mapping between the input data and the target variable, which is typically a classification label. In other words, they aim to answer the question: "Given the input data, what is the most likely class or label?"

Discriminative models are typically used for tasks such as:

* Classification (e.g., spam vs. non-spam emails)
* Regression (e.g., predicting house prices)
* Binary classification (e.g., sentiment analysis)

Examples of discriminative models include:

* Logistic Regression
* Decision Trees
* Random Forests
* Support Vector Machines (SVMs)

Generative Models:
Generative models, on the other hand, are designed to model the underlying distribution of the data. Their primary goal is to learn a probability distribution over the input data, which can be used to generate new, synthetic data that is similar to the original data. In other words, they aim to answer the question: "What is the underlying distribution of the data?"

Generative models are typically used for tasks such as:

* Data imputation (e.g., filling missing values)
* Data augmentation (e.g., generating new training data)
* Anomaly detection (e.g., identifying outliers)
* Density estimation (e.g., estimating the probability density of the data)

Examples of generative models include:

* Gaussian Mixture Models (GMMs)
* Hidden Markov Models (HMMs)
* Variational Autoencoders (VAEs)
* Generative Adversarial Networks (GANs)

Key differences:

1.   **Purpose**: Discriminative models aim to predict a specific class orlabel, while generative models aim to model the underlying distribution of the data.
2.   **Output**: Discriminative models output a probability distribution overthe classes or labels, while generative models output a probability distribution over the input data.
3.   **Training objective**: Discriminative models are typically trained using aclassification loss function (e.g., cross-entropy), while generative models are trained using a likelihood-based loss function (e.g., maximum likelihood estimation).
4.   **Applications**: Discriminative models are commonly used forclassification and regression tasks, while generative models are commonly used for data imputation, data augmentation, and anomaly detection.

In summary, discriminative models focus on predicting a specific class or label, while generative models focus on modeling the underlying distribution of the data. Both types of models have their strengths and weaknesses, and the choice of model depends on the specific problem and application.

Q: Highlight the key differences between models like GPT (Generative Pre-trained Transformer) and BERT (Bidirectional Encoder Representations from Transformers)?

A: GPT (Generative Pre-trained Transformer) and BERT (Bidirectional Encoder Representations from Transformers) are two popular language models developed by different research groups. While both models use transformer architectures, they have distinct differences in their design, training objectives, and applications.

Key differences:

1. **Training Objective:**

* GPT: Trained on a large corpus of text using a masked languagemodeling objective, where the model predicts the next word in a sequence given the context. The goal is to generate coherent and natural-sounding text.
* BERT: Trained on a large corpus of text using a combination of twoobjectives: masked language modeling and next sentence prediction. The goal is to learn contextualized representations of words and sentences.

2. **Architecture:**

* GPT: Uses a decoder-only transformer architecture, which is designed forgenerating text.
* BERT: Uses an encoder-only transformer architecture, which is designedfor encoding input text into a fixed-size representation.

3. **Directionality:**

* GPT: Trained to predict the next word in a sequence, which implies aunidirectional (left-to-right) understanding of the text.
* BERT: Trained to predict the masked word in a sentence, which allowsfor bidirectional (left-to-right and right-to-left) understanding of the text.

4. **Tokenization:**

* GPT: Uses a WordPiece tokenization scheme, which represents wordsas a combination of subwords (smaller units of words).
* BERT: Also uses a WordPiece tokenization scheme, but with a differentvocabulary size and tokenization strategy.

5. **Fine-tuning:**

* GPT: Typically fine-tuned for specific tasks like language translation, textgeneration, or text classification.
* BERT: Fine-tuned for a wide range of natural language processing (NLP)tasks, including question answering, sentiment analysis, and named entity recognition.

6. **Performance:**

* GPT: Excels at generating coherent and natural-sounding text, but maystruggle with tasks that require a deeper understanding of the input text.
* BERT: Excels at tasks that require a deep understanding of the input text,such as question answering and sentiment analysis, but may not be as effective at generating text.

In summary:

* GPT is designed for generating text and is trained using a maskedlanguage modeling objective.
* BERT is designed for encoding input text into a fixed-size representationand is trained using a combination of masked language modeling and next sentence prediction objectives.

*   While both models can be fine-tuned for specific NLP tasks, GPT is moresuited for tasks that require generating text, and BERT is more suited for tasks that require a deep understanding of the input text.

Q: What are the key differences between discriminative and generative models?

A: Discriminative and generative models are two fundamental types of machine learning models that differ in their objectives, approaches, and applications.

Discriminative Models:

Discriminative models, also known as conditional models, focus on predicting the conditional probability of a target variable given the input data. They learn to distinguish between different classes or labels by modeling the probability of a class given the input features. The goal is to learn a decision boundary that separates the classes.

Key characteristics of discriminative models:

1.   **Focus on classification**: Discriminative models are primarily used forclassification tasks, where the goal is to predict a class label or category.
2.   **Conditional probability**: They model the conditional probability of thetarget variable given the input data, $p(y|x)$.
3.   **Decision boundary**: The model learns to find the optimal decisionboundary that separates the classes.
4.   **Examples**: Logistic regression, support vector machines (SVMs), andneural networks are examples of discriminative models.

Generative Models:

Generative models, also known as joint models, focus on modeling the joint probability distribution of the input data and the target variable. They learn to generate new data samples that are similar to the training data. The goal is to learn the underlying structure of the data.
Key characteristics of generative models:

1.   **Focus on data generation**: Generative models are used for generatingnew data samples, such as images, text, or music.
2.   **Joint probability**: They model the joint probability of the input data andthe target variable, $p(x, y)$.
3.   **Data distribution**: The model learns to capture the underlyingdistribution of the data.

4.   **Examples**: Gaussian mixture models, hidden Markov models, andgenerative adversarial networks (GANs) are examples of generative models.

Key differences:

1.   **Objective**: Discriminative models focus on classification, whilegenerative models focus on data generation.
2.   **Probability modeling**: Discriminative models model the conditionalprobability, while generative models model the joint probability.
3.   **Decision boundary**: Discriminative models learn a decision boundary,while generative models learn the underlying data distribution.
4.   **Applications**: Discriminative models are commonly used forclassification, regression, and feature selection, while generative models are used for data generation, anomaly detection, and density estimation.

In summary, discriminative models are designed for classification and regression tasks, while generative models are designed for data generation and modeling the underlying structure of the data. While both types of models have their strengths and weaknesses, they are often used together to achieve better results in various applications.

Q: Explain the concept of "in-context learning" in the context of LLMs.

A: In the context of Large Language Models (LLMs), "in-context learning" refers to the ability of a model to learn from the input it receives during inference time, without the need for explicit training or fine-tuning. This means that the model can adapt to new tasks, concepts, or patterns based on the context provided in the input prompt, without requiring additional training data or updates to its weights.

In-context learning is a key feature of modern LLMs, such as transformer-based models like BERT, RoBERTa, and others. These models are designed to be highly flexible and can learn to perform a wide range of tasks, from language translation and question answering to text generation and more.

The concept of in-context learning is based on the idea that the input prompt provides sufficient information for the model to infer the task, context, or pattern that is relevant to the task at hand. The model can then use this information to generate a response that is tailored to the specific context, without requiring explicit training on that specific task.

There are several key aspects of in-context learning in LLMs:

1.   **Prompt-based learning**: The input prompt serves as a guide for the model to learn the task, context, or pattern. The prompt can be a few words, a sentence, or a longer passage, and it provides the necessary information for the model to generate a response.

2.   **Zero-shot learning**: In-context learning enables zero-shot learning, where the model can perform a task without any explicit training on that task. The model can learn to recognize patterns, relationships, and concepts based on the input prompt, without requiring additional training data.

3.   **Few-shot learning**: In-context learning also enables few-shot learning, where the model can learn to perform a task with only a few examples or instances. The model can use the input prompt to learn the task and generate a response based on the limited information provided.

4.   **Meta-learning**: In-context learning can be seen as a form of meta-learning, where the model learns to learn from the input prompt and adapt to new tasks, contexts, or patterns.

The benefits of in-context learning in LLMs include:

1.   **Improved flexibility**: In-context learning enables LLMs to adapt to a wide range of tasks and contexts, without requiring explicit training or fine-tuning.

2.   **Reduced training data**: In-context learning reduces the need for large amounts of training data, as the model can learn from the input prompt and generate a response based on that information.

3.   **Increased efficiency**: In-context learning can be more efficient than traditional training methods, as the model can learn to perform a task in a single pass, without requiring multiple iterations or updates to its weights.

However, in-context learning also has some limitations and challenges, such as:

1.   **Prompt engineering**: The quality of the input prompt can significantly impact the performance of the model. Well-designed prompts can help the model learn the task or context, while poorly designed prompts can lead to suboptimal performance.

2.   **Overfitting**: In-context learning can lead to overfitting, where the model becomes too specialized to the specific prompt or task and fails to generalize to new contexts or tasks.

3.   **Lack of interpretability**: In-context learning can make it challenging to interpret the model's decisions or understand how it arrived at a particular response, as the learning process is implicit and based on the input prompt.

Overall, in-context learning is a powerful feature of LLMs that enables them to adapt to new tasks, contexts, and patterns, without requiring explicit training or fine-tuning.

While it has many benefits, it also presents some challenges and limitations that need to be addressed through careful prompt engineering, model design, and evaluation.

Q: What are hallucinations in LLMs? how to handel it

A: Hallucinations in Large Language Models (LLMs) refer to the phenomenon where a model generates text that is not based on any actual input or context, but rather on its own internal workings or biases. This can result in the model producing text that is inaccurate, nonsensical, or unrelated to the topic at hand.

Hallucinations can occur in LLMs due to various reasons, including:

1.   **Overfitting**: When a model is trained on a limited dataset, it may learnto recognize patterns that are not generalizable to new, unseen data. As a result, the model may generate text that is based on its own internal patterns rather than the actual input.
2.   **Lack of common sense**: LLMs may not possess the same level ofcommon sense or real-world experience as humans, leading to generated text that is unrealistic or implausible.
3.   **Biases in the training data**: If the training data contains biases orinaccuracies, the model may learn to replicate these biases, resulting in hallucinated text.
4.   **Generative nature of LLMs**: LLMs are designed to generate textbased on patterns and associations learned from the training data. This can lead to the model generating text that is not grounded in reality.

To handle hallucinations in LLMs, the following strategies can be employed:
1.   **Data quality and curation**: Ensuring that the training data is accurate,diverse, and representative of the task at hand can help reduce hallucinations.
2.   **Regularization techniques**: Techniques such as dropout, weightdecay, and early stopping can help prevent overfitting and reduce hallucinations.
3.   **Incorporating external knowledge**: Providing the model with externalknowledge or constraints, such as entity recognition or fact-checking, can help ground the generated text in reality.
4.   **Human evaluation and feedback**: Having human evaluators reviewand provide feedback on the generated text can help identify and correct hallucinations.
5.   **Using hallucination detection methods**: Researchers have proposedvarious methods to detect hallucinations in LLMs, such as:
*   **Hallucination detection metrics**: Metrics like ROUGE, BLEU, andMETEOR can be used to evaluate the similarity between generated text and the reference text.

*   **Fact-checking**: Fact-checking algorithms can be used to verify theaccuracy of generated text.

*   **Uncertainty estimation**: Estimating the model's uncertainty can helpidentify when the model is likely to hallucinate.

6.   **Model architecture modifications**: Modifying the model architecture,such as using attention mechanisms or graph-based models, can help reduce hallucinations.

7.   **Ensemble methods**: Combining the outputs of multiple models canhelp reduce hallucinations by averaging out errors.

8.   **Training objectives**: Using training objectives that penalizehallucinations, such as adversarial training or reinforcement learning from human feedback, can help reduce hallucinations.

By employing these strategies, developers can reduce the likelihood of hallucinations in LLMs and improve the overall quality and reliability of generated text.

Q: What is the difference between fine tuning and training LLMs?

A: Fine-tuning and training are two distinct processes used in the development of Large Language Models (LLMs). The primary difference between them lies in their objectives, scope, and the extent of model modification. **Training:**

Training refers to the initial process of creating an LLM from scratch. This involves feeding the model a massive amount of text data, which it uses to learn patterns, relationships, and representations of language. The goal of training is to develop a model that can understand and generate human-like language. During training, the model learns to:

1. Recognize and generate text patterns
2. Understand grammar, syntax, and semantics
3. Develop a vocabulary and language representation
4. Learn to predict the next word or character in a sequence

Training is typically done on a large, diverse dataset, and the model is optimized using a loss function that measures its performance on a specific task, such as masked language modeling or next sentence prediction.

Fine-tuning:
Fine-tuning, on the other hand, is a process that takes a pre-trained LLM and adapts it to a specific task or domain. The goal of fine-tuning is to adjust the model's weights to better suit a particular application or dataset, while retaining the knowledge and representations learned during training. Fine-tuning involves:

1. Taking a pre-trained model as a starting point
2. Adding a new task-specific layer or modifying the existing architecture
3. Training the model on a smaller, task-specific dataset
4. Adjusting the model's weights to optimize performance on the target task

Fine-tuning is typically done on a smaller dataset than training, and the model is optimized using a task-specific loss function. The idea is to leverage the pre-trained model's knowledge and adapt it to the new task, rather than training a new model from scratch.

Key differences:

1.   **Objective:** Training aims to develop a general-purpose languagemodel, while fine-tuning aims to adapt the model to a specific task or domain.
2.   **Scope:** Training involves learning from a large, diverse dataset, whilefine-tuning involves learning from a smaller, task-specific dataset.
3.   **Model modification:** Training involves creating a new model fromscratch, while fine-tuning involves modifying an existing pre-trained model. 4. **Computational resources:** Training typically requires more computational resources than fine-tuning, as it involves processing large amounts of data and optimizing a larger number of model parameters.

In summary, training is the process of creating an LLM from scratch, while fine-tuning is the process of adapting a pre-trained LLM to a specific task or domain. Both processes are essential in the development of LLMs, and they are often used in conjunction with each other to achieve state-of-the-art results in natural language processing tasks.

www.ingramcontent.com/pod-product-compliance
Lightning Source LLC
LaVergne TN
LVHW051325050326
832903LV00031B/3372